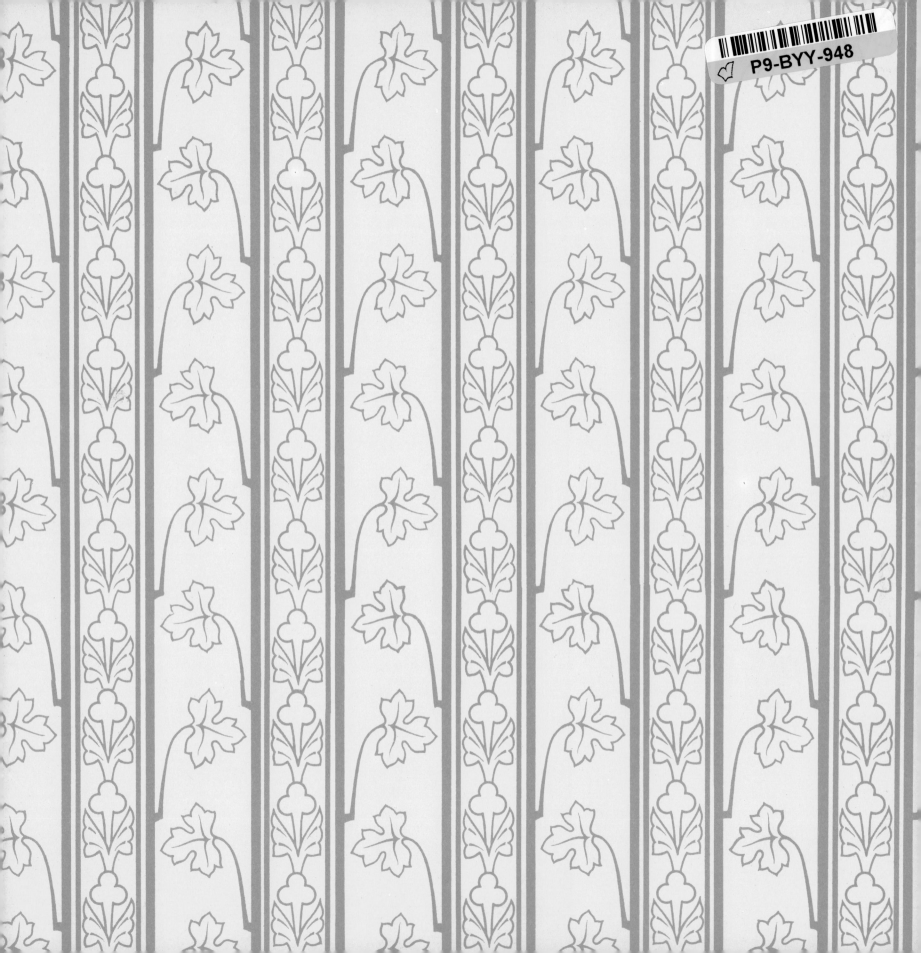

P9-BYY-948

GREAT AMERICAN HOTELS

Luxury Palaces and Elegant Resorts

GREAT AMERICAN HOTELS
Luxury Palaces and Elegant Resorts

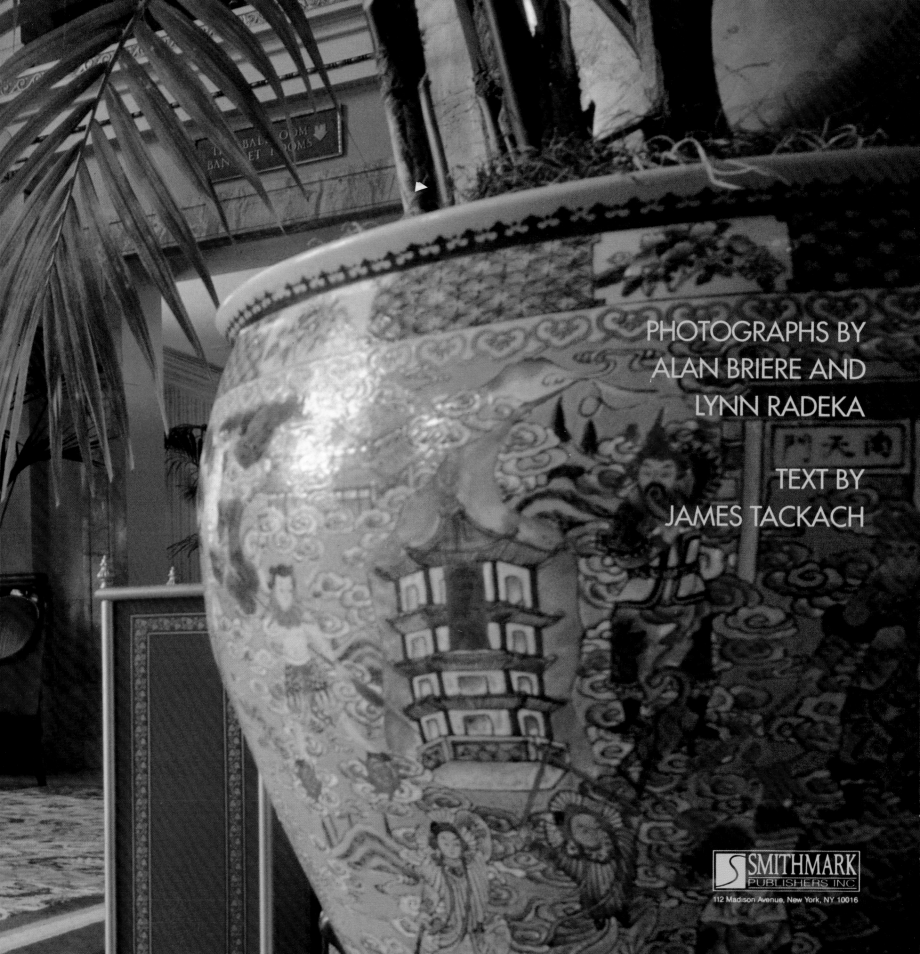

PHOTOGRAPHS BY
ALAN BRIERE AND

LYNN RADEKA

TEXT BY

JAMES TACKACH

SMITHMARK
PUBLISHERS INC

112 Madison Avenue, New York, NY 10016

SMITHMARK
PUBLISHERS INC.
112 Madison Avenue, New York, NY 10016

AN M&M BOOK

Copyright © 1991 by M & M Books
ISBN 0-8317-3929-0
All rights reserved

Great American Hotels was prepared and produced by M & M Books, 11 W. 19th Street, New York, New York 10011.

Project Director & Editor Gary Fishgall

Editorial Assistants Maxine Dormer, Ben D'Amprisi, Jr.; **Copyediting** Bert N. Zelman, Keith Walsh of Publishers Workshop; **Proofreading** Shirley Vierheller.

Designer Marcy Stamper

Separations and Printing Regent Publishing Services Ltd.

First published in the United States in 1991 by Smithmark Publishers, Inc., 112 Madison Avenue, New York, New York 10016.

Smithmark Books are available for bulk purchase for sales promotions and premium use. For details, write or telephone the Manager of Special Sales, Smithmark Publishers, Inc. 112 Madison Avenue, New York, New York 10016, (212) 532-6600.

Previous pages The lobby of the Willard Inter-Continental Hotel, Washington, D.C.

These pages The gardens of the Grand Hotel, Mackinac Island, Michigan.

Alan Briere All photos on pages 8–71, front jacket *(upper right, lower right, lower center)*, pages 2–3, 4–5, 7, and 128.

Lynn Radeka All photos on pages 72–127, front jacket *(upper left, upper center, lower left)*, page 6, and back jacket.

All black-and-white photos courtesy of the respective hotels except for that on page 19, which was provided by Color Library Books and page 53, which was provided by the *Courier-Journal*.

Contents

Introduction

ALTHOUGH THE WORD "HOTEL" is French in origin, referring originally to any large building, the hotel as we know it today is an American invention of the late-18th century. The hotel's ancestor, the inn, is, of course, thousands of years old. From the time human beings built civilizations, innkeepers rented rooms for the night to weary travelers and offered food and drink to make journeys more bearable. Hundreds of folk tales, myths, and Bible stories are built around city and roadside inns.

The pre-19th-century inn, however, resembles the modern hotel only in its central purpose—to provide a traveler with a place to spend a night. Inns were generally fairly small, sometimes merely a few rooms occupying a floor above the innkeeper's own living quarters. And though the modern bed-and-breakfast inn might afford a guest all the contemporary amenities, the inns of yesteryear often provided only the most basic of accommodations. Private rooms were not the norm, and a guest was often required to share a bed with one or more strangers.

Large, multi-room lodging houses offering guests all the comforts of home are less than 200 years old. The first such building to be called a "hotel" opened in 1794, a 73-room lodge on Broadway in New York City that the proprietor named the "City Hotel." It became the talk of the town and an important Knickerbocker social center. After the turn of the century, large lodging houses, not always called "hotels," appeared in other cities—the Exchange Coffee House in Boston, the Mansion House in Philadelphia, the City Hotel in Baltimore.

America's first "grand hotel," one that boasted opulent decor and luxury accommodations, was Boston's Tremont House, a four-story edifice fronted by stately columns that opened in 1829. The 173-room lodge offered features that no other American hotel, and certainly no inn, could match—a marble-floored lobby, carpeted guests rooms, a massive formal dining hall. Visitors to Boston in the 1830s were said to have demanded a tour of Tremont House before taking in other Boston landmarks like the Old North Church and the State House. Soon luxury hotels like Tremont House sprouted in other American cities.

THE BEVERLY HILLS HOTEL

It is not surprising that Americans would invent the hotel, because such a lodging place combines two essential, though contradictory, aspects of the American character—the impulse to build closely-knit communities, a trait inherited from the early Pilgrim and Puritan settlers, and the impulse to travel, part of the pioneer spirit that helped Americans conquer their continent. The hotel is essentially designed to meet the needs of the traveler, the pioneer; but in its open public rooms, its dining halls and cafes, and its shops and gardens, guests can get a sense of community that is unattainable at a roadside inn.

Within 50 years of the opening of Tremont House, all major American cities and many towns and hamlets had hotels. The great post-Civil War urban migration created the need for temporary lodging in big cities. The increase in leisure time available to Americans who moved off the farm and the expansion of the

THE WILLARD INTER-CONTINENTAL HOTEL

railroad across the continent—both of which helped spawn the country's vacation industry—further necessitated the need for lodging places. And by the 1870s, the idea of the hotel had crossed the Atlantic and taken hold in Europe.

Today, of course, the telephone directory of even the smallest American town might list two or three hotels. The phone book of a major city would list dozens. The 15 hotels highlighted in this book, however, are very special lodging places. All these are "grand hotels," those that boast the finest in architecture, interior decor, and comforts. Their lobbies have large chandeliers and rich carpeting; guest rooms have marble baths and luxurious furnishings. They also have large staffs specially trained to pamper their patrons with regal service. Most hotels are in the business of accommodating guests; these hotels practice the art of hostelry.

THIS BOOK INVITES ITS READERS to visit these luxury lodging places. The text will offer a brief description of each hotel—its architectural style, its history, its amenities—and the splendid photographs by Alan Briere and Lynn Radeka, all of which were taken specifically for this volume, will provide a first-hand look at its exterior, lobbies, guest rooms, and facilities. While the text tells you *about* the hotel, the photos beckon you to enter its grounds—to stand before it and admire its style, to enter its lobby and relax in one of its inviting nooks, to peruse its sumptuous shops, and to enjoy its food and drink. And, if you're lucky, to sample its accommodations.

Selecting the 15 hostelries for this book was a difficult task because there are many fine hotels around the country. Certainly the Waldorf-Astoria in New York, the Fairmount in San Francisco, and the Royal Orleans in New Orleans were worthy of consideration. But limits of space and the desire to provide geographic diversity among the hotels precluded their inclusion.

Those that were chosen vary in age—from the 120-year-old Mohonk Mountain House to the 25-year-old Caesars Palace—and in architectural styles—from the ornate Beaux Arts Plaza Hotel in New York City to the simple log cabin style of the Old Faithful Inn. They are located in bustling metropolitan centers and in sleepy mountain resorts. They are owned by large conglomerates and by individual families.

They are more alike, however, than they are different, because each in its own way seeks to provide quality service in a splendid setting. Like other great buildings—the United States Capitol; Monticello, Thomas Jefferson's home; the Brooklyn Bridge—they have become symbols. They recall the history of by-gone eras, they introduce us to the genius of their creators, and they capture and reflect the locales in which they serve. Moreover, they exemplify a tradition of gracious living, enjoyed by relatively few, and a continuing standard of excellence that is increasingly rare in this hectic, technology-laden world. They are America's great hotels.

THE PLAZA

The Mohonk Mountain House
New Paltz, New York

MANY OF AMERICA'S GREAT LANDMARKS—the Brooklyn Bridge, the Hoover Dam, the Empire State Building—are monuments to progress. The Mohonk Mountain House, a 120-year-old lodge hugging Lake Mohonk in New York's Shawangunk Mountains, however, stands as a symbol of a more tranquil time, before the great technological changes of the 20th century took place.

The Mohonk Mountain House, located in New Paltz, New York, a short drive from Poughkeepsie, sits atop a mountain ridge that has not been substantially altered since glaciers moved through the area some 12,000 years ago, creating the region's lakes and its rugged range of shale and quartz cliffs and hilltops. The hotel grounds include thousands of acres of unsullied forest land, covered by white pines and hardwoods and inhabited by deer and other wildlife. The adjoining Mohonk Preserve and Minnewaska State Park bring the total of protected wilderness land surrounding the hotel to 24,000 acres. At the foot of the hotel is glistening Lake Mohonk, the only one of the area's five glacial bodies of water not ruined by acid rain.

The hotel's ownership has also remained unchanged. From its opening on June 1, 1870, to the present, the Mohonk Mountain House has been run by members of the Smiley family, originally of Maine. In 1869, Alfred Smiley, who had previously moved his family to a farm in Poughkeepsie, took a horseback ride to Lake Mohonk and lodged at Stokes Tavern, the area's only hotel. He liked the region so much that he offered to buy the tavern, the lake, and 300 surrounding acres from the proprietor, John F. Stokes. When they reached a tentative agreement, Smiley notified his twin brother, Albert, a Providence, Rhode Island, schoolteacher, and the two men became partners in the hotel business. They remodeled Stokes Tavern, changed its name, and opened for business the following spring. Being strict Quakers, the Smileys prohibited alcohol and gambling at their new lodge, which they billed as a respite from the noise and commotion of city life. The

▲ THIS CLOSE-UP VIEW OF THE CENTRAL STAIRCASE REVEALS THE WORK OF A SKILLED CRAFTSMAN.

◄ THE MOHONK MOUNTAIN HOUSE, WHICH OPENED IN 1870, RESEMBLES A MAGICAL MEDIEVAL CASTLE SET ON THE SHORES OF A GLISTENING LAKE.

THIS CENTRAL STAIRWAY, MADE OF SOLID HARDWOODS, CARRIES GUESTS FROM THE LOBBY TO THE UPPER FLOORS.

Smileys charged guests from $14 to $20 per week to stay at their hotel, and dinner was provided for an additional $1.50. One hundred and twenty years later, the tariffs are substantially higher, but the Smiley family still owns Mohonk Mountain House, under the corporate name of Smiley Brothers Inc.

THE 40-ROOM GUEST HOUSE that Alfred and Albert opened in 1870 has been greatly expanded. From 1879 through 1902, the Smiley brothers, with the assistance of their architect, James E. Ware, added several buildings to the original structure to house additional guest rooms, a new

kitchen and dining room, and a large formal public parlor. The result was a rambling Victorian structure whose tile-topped turrets, multichimneyed roofs, and dozens of balconies and connecting bridges were more reminiscent of a magical medieval castle than a hotel. Today Mohonk Mountain House, with its asymmetrical shape and eclectic building materials, recalls all the spontaneity and whimsy of the Victorian era.

Although the hotel has been greatly expanded, its interior has retained its original 19th-century charm. The splendid Parlor Wing, which fronts the hotel's seven-story central building and overhangs Lake Mohonk, is richly

THE STONE OBSERVATION TOWER WAS BUILT AS A MEMORIAL TO ALBERT SMILEY, ONE OF THE HOTEL'S FOUNDERS. THE TOWER'S IRON GATE WITH ITS SPLENDID OVERVIEW OF THE HUDSON RIVER VALLEY IS SEEN IN THE PICTURE ON THE OPPOSITE PAGE.

paneled and warmed by large stone fireplaces. Guests can relax in wicker rockers and soft easy chairs—and much of the parlor furniture is original. In many of the hotel's 281 guest rooms are wood-burning fireplaces to ward off chilly mountain nights. The long corridors throughout the hotel are decorated with tasteful Victorian, Adirondack, and Mission-style furnishings, as well as turn-of-the-century photographs and artwork that bring contemporary guests back to an earlier time.

A special attraction is Mohonk Mountain House's magnificent main dining room, two stories high and accented with bracketed wooden columns. Rows of clerestory windows pour light into the eating area, and hardwood floors, tables, and chairs help create the rustic atmosphere desired by so many of the hotel's patrons. But atmosphere is not the dining room's only attraction. The chefs at Mohonk Mountain House pride themselves on their tasty, healthy, natural meals and snacks.

THE MOHONK MOUNTAIN HOUSE'S grounds are as appealing as the fine hotel. In 1886, Albert Smiley began work on the splendid flower garden that fronts the lodge. Modeled on the magnificent show gardens of Victorian estates, Smiley's creation provides guests with a serene and picturesque setting for a morning stroll or a late afternoon repose. Mohonk Mountain House lodgers can also enjoy the fragrant herb garden, the wildflower

THROUGHOUT THE HOTEL, THE FURNISHINGS ARE STYLISHLY UNDERSTATED. ONE OF THE HOTEL'S TOWER ROOMS IS PICTURED HERE.

and fern trail, and the many wisteria trees and vine-covered arbors that surround the hotel. Other attractions on the grounds include several working greenhouses; the stables and Barn Museum, a large, multi winged structure that houses 19th-century carriages, old blacksmith tools, and antique cars; an agriculture museum; and dozens of gazebos and towers built on nearby hilltops to afford hikers splendid views of the Shawangunk Mountains.

But one of the most appealing features of the Mohonk Mountain House is its mission, the philosophical agenda set by the Smiley brothers and still carried out today. Earnest Quakers, the Smileys wanted to offer guests more than good hospitality; they sought to provide a peaceful and healthy environment where lodgers could rest their bodies and enrich their minds. The hotel still offers dozens of educational programs and

AS THIS 19TH-CENTURY ILLUSTRATION INDICATES, THE MOHONK'S GROUNDS, DEVELOPED BY ALBERT SMILEY BEGINNING IN 1886, PROVIDED SERENE AND PICTURESQUE SETTINGS FOR STROLLS AND QUIET TETE-A-TETES.

This second-floor parlor provides a rich setting for meetings, lectures, and other public events.

hosts conferences on world peace. Prayer services are held on Sundays. Tennis courts, hiking and cross-country ski trails, and a fitness center encourage guests to enjoy a healthy physical work-out during their stay. Smoking is prohibited in public rooms, and alcoholic beverages, banned until 1965, are served only in the dining halls and guest rooms. In the evening, jackets and ties are required of male guests in the dining room, and motorists are urged to drive "slowly and quietly, please." Only three television sets can be found on the premises.

While many great 19th-century hotels have changed with the times, the Mohonk Mountain House, now a National Historic Landmark, has worked hard to remain as it was a century ago. Its philosophy, its unique architecture, and its glorious setting combine to make this mountain lodge one of America's great hostelries.

THE HOTEL'S SOUTH PORCH OFFERS GUESTS A FINE VIEW OF LAKE MOHONK.

The Plaza
New York, New York

NEW YORK IS A SPRAWLING METROPOLIS of nearly eight million people and 365 square miles comprising America's financial center, its most important theater district, and its busiest seaport. New York is also the home of great museums, world-famous restaurants, and grand hotels, the grandest of which is the Plaza at Fifth Avenue and Central Park South. As the hotel's brochures suggest, the Plaza is "New York at its best."

The Plaza is the creation of four men: George Fuller, the founder of the Fuller Construction Company; Harry St. Francis Black, Fuller's son-in-law and this company's president; Bernhard Beinecke, a hotel owner and financier; and John W. Gates, the Illinois farmboy who made a fortune manufacturing barbed wire. In 1902, these men pur-

chased a large but bland 15-year-old hotel on Fifth Avenue and Central Park South—also called the Plaza—and decided to replace it with one that would be the most magnificent structure of its kind in New York City, a grand edifice

◄ THE PLAZA, A FRENCH RENAISSANCE-STYLE MASTERPIECE OVERLOOKING NEW YORK'S CENTRAL PARK, OPENED IN 1907.

▲ THIS MURAL, REMINISCENT OF THE ROCOCO STYLE OF WATTEAU AND BOUCHER, ADORNS A WALL IN ONE OF THE PLAZA'S MEETING ROOMS.

that would reflect the power, energy, and elegance of the great metropolis. They enlisted as their architect Henry

Janeway Hardenbergh, who had designed New York's original Waldorf-Astoria Hotel, Boston's Copley Plaza, and the majestic Dakota Apartments on Manhattan's 72nd Street and Central Park West.

Hardenbergh envisioned a Beaux Arts palace in the French Renaissance style, a hotel that would complement the magnificent buildings in the area—Cornelius Vanderbilt's 100-room chateau between 57th and 58th Streets; St. Patrick's Cathedral, several blocks away on Fifth Avenue; and an impressive string of townhouses, villas, and galleries. Construction began in 1905, and the new Plaza opened on October 1, 1907. It cost $12 million, a staggering sum at the turn of the century.

But when the doors opened, New York had a most impressive new addi-

THE EDWARDIAN ROOM, PICTURED HERE, OFFERS A SPLENDID TURN-OF-THE-CENTURY ATMOSPHERE, A FIVE-STAR MENU, AND AN AWESOME VIEW OF CENTRAL PARK.

▲ THE BATHROOM OF THE VANDERBILT SUITE OFFERS PATRONS A TUB AND JACUZZI, A PLACE TO RELAX AFTER AN ARDUOUS DAY ON THE STREETS OF NEW YORK.

▶ ARCHITECT HENRY J. HARDENBERGH NOT ONLY DESIGNED THE PLAZA BUT ALSO NEW YORK'S ORIGINAL WALDORF-ASTORIA HOTEL AND BOSTON'S COPLEY PLAZA.

tion to its already fine array of hotels. Perched at the edge of Central Park, the Plaza stood 19 stories high, a skyscraper at the turn of the century. The bottom three stories were built of marble and accented with stately columns and wide balconies. Above the third floor, Hardenbergh used granite. The top six floors were a lavish collection of gables, turrets, and balconies—a magnificent crown that dominated the Central Park

skyline. The decor included expensive Savonnerie rugs, imported Louis XVI furniture, gold-encrusted china, and fine Irish linens.

THE NEW HOTEL soon became the talk of New York, thanks in part to Fred Sterry, one of the nation's career hotel managers, brought in by Gates to serve as the Plaza's general manager. Dozens of the city's most famous socialites paid a visit or rented rooms—Vanderbilts and Goulds; "Diamond Jim" Brady and his consort, Lillian Russell; Samuel Clemens, better known by his pen name, Mark Twain; and Enrico Caruso, the great Italian opera singer. During the 1920s, the Plaza became the hangout of Scott and Zelda Fitzgerald, Ernest Hemingway, George M. Cohan, and other Jazz Age notables. Frank Lloyd Wright lived at the Plaza from 1953 to 1959, while the Guggenheim Museum was under construction. Although Beaux Arts buildings ran counter to his tastes, the great architect enjoyed staying at the Plaza, saying, "I like it almost as much as if I'd built it myself." Over the years, the hotel has also been used as a setting for more than a score of noteworthy films, including *North by Northwest, Funny Girl, Breakfast at Tiffany's, Barefoot in the Park, The Great Gatsby, Crocodile Dundee,* and, of course, *Plaza Suite.*

THE BRIGHT LIGHTS AND LUSH GREENERY OF THE PALM COURT, LOCATED AT THE CENTER OF THE MAIN LOBBY, SUGGEST THE ATMOSPHERE OF A EUROPEAN OUTDOOR CAFÉ.

▶ DONALD
TRUMP,
CURRENT
OWNER OF THE
PLAZA.

THE OAK ROOM,
NAMED FOR
ITS STYLISH
WOODWORK, IS
ONE OF NEW
YORK'S MOST
ELEGANT
EATERIES.

Today, the Plaza is still the place
to be for the movers and shakers of
New York society as well as business
leaders and dignitaries from across the
globe. The hotel has been splendidly
preserved, and restoration is an ongo-
ing process. The lobby and public
rooms retain their Gilded Age opulence, offering frazzled New Yorkers
and visitors to the Big Apple a temporary respite from the noise and commotion of the city's streets. The lobby
is furnished with antique marble tables
topped by colorful floral arrangements. The lobby corridors have
recently been recarpeted, refurnished,
repainted, and gilded and missing wall
and ceiling moldings have been
replaced and restored.

AT THE CENTER OF THE MAIN LOBBY is the Palm Court, one of New York's most famous eating and meeting places. Built with Caen stone and marble and enclosed with large arched windows, the Palm Court remains an ideal setting for a business lunch or elegant Sunday brunch. Large palms set in antique plant holders suggest the atmosphere of a breezy outdoor café.

In addition to the Palm Court, the Plaza houses four other eateries. The Edwardian Room offers breakfast, lunch, and dinner in a turn-of-the-century atmosphere. The Oak Room is one of New York's most famous hotel restaurants. Its 25-foot-high ceiling is supported by sturdy oak columns, and its walls are adorned with oak panels and hand-painted murals. Once the favorite lunch and dinner spot of the area's stockbrokers, as well as the dining place of choice for George M. Cohan's theater entourage, the Oak Room continues to serve hearty American lunches and dinners in its classic setting. The adjoining Oak Bar, which was rented as office space by E. F. Hutton during Prohibition, presents patrons with a grand view of Central Park as they enjoy lunch and light supper. The Oyster Bar, a traditional English pub with etched-glass windows and a copper-topped bar, serves seafood

THE VANDERBILT SUITE IS ONE OF THE PLAZA'S 16 SPECIALTY SUITES. MANHATTAN OFFERS FEW, IF ANY, MORE LUXURIOUS LODGINGS.

specialties with an extensive selection of imported beers and ales.

The Plaza's 815 guest rooms are individually decorated, featuring handsome crystal chandeliers, marble baths, and in some cases their original marble fireplaces. The hotel also contains 96 suites and 16 specialty suites, including the massive Presidential Suite with four bedrooms, two living rooms, a dining room and kitchen, four baths, a wine cellar, and servants' quarters; the Vanderbilt Suite, with Jacuzzi and marble fireplace; and the Frank Lloyd Wright Suite, which contains a gallery of Wright's prints and sketches and reproductions of the great architect's furniture, fabrics, and tableware. Also on the hotel's premises are a barber shop, a beauty salon, a movie theater, and an array of fine shops.

Designated a National Historic Landmark in 1986, the Plaza is now owned and operated by the Trump Organization. After eight decades of operation, the hotel retains its reputation as New York's premier hostelry — an imposing edifice which captures the history, verve, and splendor of a great American city.

MANY OF THE FURNISHINGS, TABLEWARE, AND FABRICS IN THE FRANK LLOYD WRIGHT SUITE ARE REPRODUCTIONS OF THE ARCHITECT'S ORIGINAL DESIGNS.

The Willard Inter-Continental Hotel
Washington, D.C.

• • •

IN JULY 1968, the Willard Hotel, a turn-of-the-century Beaux Arts masterpiece on Pennsylvania Avenue in Washington, D.C., closed its splendid doors for business. For the next 18 years, the hotel was vacant, and only court orders and the site's listing in the National Register of Historical Places saved it from the wrecker's ball. Fortunately, individuals with respect for history and tradition gained control of the hotel and saw to it that the Willard was preserved and restored. In August 1986, the Willard reopened its doors to overnight guests. In a very short time, the hotel was again one of the capital city's finest lodging places.

The Willard was worth saving — even just for history's sake. The piece of Pennsylvania Avenue occupied by the great hotel had been the site of a hostelry of some

sort since 1816, when Colonel John Tayloe built a row of three-story residences and offered rooms to travelers. His inn became known first as Man-

▲ THE WILLARD'S MAGNIFICENT LOBBY, BEDECKED WITH RICH CARPETS AND STYLISH VICTORIAN FURNISHINGS, RECALLS AMERICA'S GILDED AGE DURING THE LATE 19TH AND EARLY 20TH CENTURIES.

◀ THE WILLARD INTER-CONTINENTAL HOTEL, WHICH OPENED IN 1904, WAS DESIGNED BY HENRY JANEWAY HARDENBERGH, THE TURN-OF-THE-CENTURY'S MOST FAMOUS HOTEL ARCHITECT.

sion House and later as the City Hotel. In 1850, Henry Willard bought the place, renamed it for himself, remod-

eled it, and built a large addition, making the hotel one of the most attractive in the city. President Franklin Pierce used the Willard Hotel for state dinners, and President-elect Abraham Lincoln stayed there until his inauguration (upon his arrival in the city, he was secretly escorted to the hotel from the train station in response to assassination threats; with his first presidential paycheck he paid his bill of $773.75).

Throughout the Civil War, the Willard was at the center of Washington's social and political life. In 1861, Julia Ward Howe composed the stirring Civil War anthem, "The Battle Hymn of the Republic," while staying at the Willard. In 1862, Nathaniel Hawthorne, the great novelist and short story writer, stayed at the hotel while he toured the Virginia battlefields, and he claimed that he received a better sense of the war at

the hotel than at the army barracks he visited. "This hotel, in fact," wrote Hawthorne in *Atlantic Monthly*, "may be much more justly called the center of Washington and the Union than either the Capitol, the White House or the State Department. . . . Never, in another place, was there such a miscellany of people. You exchange nods with governors of sovereign States; you elbow illustrious men, and tread on the toes of generals; you hear statesmen and orators speaking in their familiar tones." After the war, President Ulysses Grant used the Willard's lobby as a temporary escape from the pressures of the White

▲ THE OLD WILLARD HOTEL CAN BE SEEN AT LEFT, FLYING THE AMERICAN FLAG, IN THIS ILLUSTRATION OF ABRAHAM LINCOLN'S JOURNEY TO THE CAPITOL BUILDING FOR HIS INAUGURATION ON MARCH 4, 1861. LINCOLN STAYED AT THE HOTEL AS PRESIDENT-ELECT.

▶ THE ROUND ROBIN BAR IS A REPLICA OF THE WILLARD'S ORIGINAL LOUNGE FOR MEN ONLY, WHERE, ACCORDING TO LEGEND, SENATOR HENRY CLAY INTRODUCED THE MINT JULEP TO WASHINGTON.

(LEFT) A GARRET WINDOW IN THE JENNY LIND SUITE OFFERS GUESTS A BIRD'S-EYE VIEW OF THE WASHINGTON MONUMENT.

(RIGHT) A CLOSE-UP VIEW OF THE CAPITAL SUITE'S DINING ROOM, WITH ITS STENCILED WALL TRIM AND FRAMED STILL LIFE PAINTING, EXEMPLIFIES THE WILLARD'S CAREFULLY ORCHESTRATED DECOR.

House. Legend has it that he coined the term "lobbyist" in reference to the many people who gave him advice and asked for favors in the Willard's lobby.

Late in the 19th century the hotel underwent a series of renovations and cosmetic changes and, as the new century dawned, Willard decided that a new structure was warranted. Construction, which began in 1900, was executed in two stages so that the Willard could remain open throughout. The

A RAISED CANOPY BED DOMINATES THE
BEDROOM IN THE HONEYMOON, OR
JENNY LIND, SUITE.

The Willard now houses 365 guest rooms, each featuring fine reproduction furnishings, and 37 suites, the most elegant being the Presidential Suite, with its marble foyer and stately oval dining room, and the Jenny Lind Suite, which is furnished to resemble a French garret and offers a grand view of the Washington Monument. The hotel also houses fine eateries, including the Willard Room, one of Washington's most elegant restaurants, and Café Espresso, which offers light meals in an informal setting. Cocktails are served at the Round Robin Bar and at the Nest, a peaceful lounge on the Willard's top floor that affords patrons a bird's-eye view of Pennsylvania Avenue. The Willard boasts 13 meeting rooms, including the impressive Main Ballroom and the lavish Crystal Room.

Today, the Willard is the North American flagship of the Inter-Continental Hotels Corporation. Located in the heart of Washington, it affords guests a short walk or transit ride to the White House, the Washington Monument, the Lincoln Memorial, and the other attractions of the nation's capital.

THE BATHROOM OF THE CAPITAL SUITE.

The Greenbrier
White Sulphur Springs, West Virginia

THE GREENBRIER SERVES AS TESTIMONY to the enduring qualities of the antebellum South. This magnificent hotel is actually the second hostelry to serve as a centerpiece for the resort cottages that sprung up in the early 19th century around White Sulphur Springs, West Virginia. The first, affectionately called "the Old White," opened in 1858 and was razed in 1922. This three-story, dome-topped hotel fronted by a columned porch served as a bastion of refinement in the 19th-century South. Confederate generals dined there—Robert E. Lee summered at the Old White after the Civil War—and Virginia debutantes met their future husbands at its elegant balls.

The Greenbrier, built in 1913 by the Chesapeake & Ohio Railway Company, which owned most of the White Sulphur Springs resort, was designed in the same antebellum style. Frederick J. Sterner, a New York architect, created a fitting companion for the Old White, a seven-story, 250-room hotel in the Georgian style that gave evidence to the survival of Southern culture after the Civil War. No visitor to the Greenbrier would believe that the Old South was "gone with the wind."

With its magnificent five-story columned portico, Sterner's immaculate white hotel resembled an oversized Southern plantation house. Flowering trees, neatly trimmed shrubbery, and colorful gardens fronted the building, enticing guests to enter its doors and step back in time. Once inside, patrons entered a majestic lobby with soaring ceilings, tasteful Southern furnishings, and a splendid fireplace.

Through the 1920s, the Greenbrier continued to attract men and women of fashion who sought the peace and solitude of the Allegheny Mountains and the healing waters of the many nearby hot springs. President Woodrow Wilson, Thomas Edison, General John Pershing, and the Prince of Wales, later Edward III, were among

▲ THE PINK WALLS OF THE GREENBRIER'S MAIN BALLROOM ARE ACCENTED WITH WHITE TRIM AND OFFSET BY DEEP RED CARPETING AND FURNITURE COVERINGS. THE RESULT, ENHANCED BY THE RICH CEILING MOLDING AND BRILLIANT CHANDELIER, IS QUITE REGAL.

◀ THE GREENBRIER, WHICH OPENED IN 1913, WAS BUILT IN THE STYLE OF AN ANTEBELLUM SOUTHERN MANSION.

the distinguished guests. In 1930, three new wings were added to Sterner's original building to meet the demand for additional lodging space.

The Greenbrier survived the Great Depression as many wealthy Americans closed or lost their vacation estates and summered instead in White Sulphur Springs. Then, in the winter of 1941/42, the resort was used as an internment facility for German and Japanese diplomats awaiting exchange for American envoys detained abroad. The Greenbrier reopened for the summer; but on September 1, 1942, it was purchased by the U.S. Government and converted to a 2,200-bed hospital for soldiers wounded during World War II.

AFTER THE WAR, the C&O Railway repurchased the Greenbrier and began the arduous task of restoring the hotel to its former glory. Dorothy Draper, a noted interior designer, was hired to oversee the project. Lobbies and corridors were rearranged; ballrooms and dining halls were remodeled. Most of the Greenbrier's furnishings had been sold when the U.S. Army moved in, so authentic antiques and quality reproductions had to be acquired to re-create the flavor of the Old South. In April 1948, a reopening party was held, and the guests included the Duke and Duchess of Windsor, Mr. and Mrs. John Jacob Astor, Bing Crosby, and Congressman John F. Kennedy. The Greenbrier was once again open for business.

In subsequent years, the hotel was again expanded. The West Wing

THIS ELEGANT STAIRWAY WITH ITS ORNATELY DETAILED BANNISTER LEADS TO THE UPPER-FLOOR GUEST ROOMS.

was added in 1954, and the West Virginia Wing was built eight years later, eventually giving the main hotel a total of 650 guest rooms, 51 luxury suites, and several dining rooms and lounges, meeting rooms, and lobbies. The Greenbrier, however, comprises more than just the fine hotel designed by Frederick Sterner in 1913 and its additions. The entire complex includes 6,500 acres of land, a conference center, a clinic offering expert medical services, a cooking school, and 69 guest cottages.

SOME OF THE GREENBRIER'S COTTAGES are among the resort's oldest accommodations. The Paradise Row and Alabama Row cottages, built in the early 1800s, are still used today, some as the Greenbrier's Creative Art Colony and some as luxury guest houses. The Baltimore Row bungalows date to 1832, and Tansas Row was built in 1858. Older cottages have, of course, been masterfully restored, and new ones have been

▲ NEOCLASSICAL STATUARY LIKE THE BUST PICTURED HERE CALLS TO MIND THE ELEGANCE OF THE PLANTATION HOUSES OF THE OLD SOUTH.

▼ THE DUCHESS OF WINDSOR PRESENTS A CHECK TO GOLFER SAM SNEAD, WINNER OF THE TOURNAMENT IN THE GREENBRIER'S 1953 SPRING FESTIVAL, AS THE DUKE OF WINDSOR (RIGHT) BEAMS.

AN INTIMATE CORNER OF THE POOLSIDE LOUNGE.

THE CONFECTIONERY-COLORED SPRING
ROOM, WITH ITS PLEASING BLEND OF
PINK, WHITE, AND GREEN, PROVIDES A
RESTFUL SETTING FOR AN INFORMAL
RECEPTION.

added. Most are fronted with covered porches, giving guests the feeling of the Old South; yet the furnishings and amenities—cable television, wet bars, large baths—offer all the comforts of the present day.

The Greenbrier cottage that attracts the most attention is the President's Cottage Museum, located a short walk from the main hotel. This two-story colonnaded home, built in 1835 by Stephen Henderson, a wealthy New Orleans sugar planter, became the "summer White House" of Presidents Martin

Van Buren, John Tyler, Millard Fillmore, Franklin Pierce, and James Buchanan. The structure, preserved with great care, now serves as a museum housing antique furnishings and memorabilia from the presidents and other important guests of the Greenbrier.

Today's lodgers are very different from those of decades past. The pre-Civil War patrons of the Old White might have been content to spend their afternoons on the hotel's splendid porch conversing and sipping cool drinks. But the Greenbrier's current guests, whether they be busy executives attending a conference or vacationers enjoying a week or two of leisure, are often active sportsmen and sportswomen. For them, the Greenbrier offers an array of athletic activities matched by only a few American resorts. Three championship golf courses—including the Greenbrier Course, which was recently redesigned by Jack Nicklaus—offer golfers the challenges of the PGA tour. Fifteen outdoor and five indoor tennis courts and two platform tennis courts accommodate racquet players. Indoor and outdoor Olympic-size pools, jogging paths, and hiking and cross-country ski trails serve serious exercise enthusiasts. There are also facilities for skeet and trap shooting, bowling, skating, and fishing. After a rigorous workout, guests can be pampered by the staff of the Greenbrier Spa and Mineral Baths.

The Greenbrier, designated a National Historic Landmark in 1990, is owned by the CSX Corporation. Its staff of 1,600 employees, serving a maximum of 1,200 guests, continues the noble tradition of Southern hospitality begun at the resort almost two centuries ago.

THE GREENBRIER'S GARDENS AND GROUNDS ARE BEDECKED WITH STATUES LIKE THE ONE PICTURED HERE.

The Breakers
Palm Beach, Florida

"MY DOMAIN BEGINS AT JACKSONVILLE," claimed Henry Morrison Flagler, a co-founder with John D. Rockefeller of Standard Oil. Flagler's claim was only a slight exaggeration. The oil magnate who had left his family's farm in Hopewell, New York, with nine cents in his pocket had, by the year 1900, either owned or helped develop a good portion of the profitable vacation land on Florida's east coast.

Born in 1830, Flagler had left home at the age of 14 to work for a relative in Ohio. He saved his money, which he invested in a salt mine in the 1850s, but that business went bankrupt after the Civil War. Later he went to work for Rockefeller's fledgling oil company in Cleveland. In 1870, Rockefeller, Flagler, and Samuel Andrews formed Standard Oil and soon became wealthy men.

In the late 1870s, Flagler began spending winters in St. Augustine, Florida, because of his wife's poor health. Flagler loved the old Spanish town, but he found the region was too uncivilized for his taste. St. Augustine had one decent hotel, the St. James, and transportation to and from the area was atrocious. Flagler reasoned that if Florida's transportation system could be improved,

the state's entire east coast might become very inviting to well-to-do Northerners like himself who hated cold winters. Indeed, he came to see the whole east coast of Florida as valuable resort real estate just waiting for shrewd investors to step in.

Flagler began investing in 1885, after he retired as an active executive with Standard Oil. In March, he bought several acres of property in the middle of St. Augustine and hired Thomas Hastings and John Carrère, the New York architects who had designed the U.S. Senate building and the New York Public Library, to plan a lavish Spanish-style hotel. The magnificent Ponce de León Hotel (now a part of Flagler College) opened in 1888. Even before it was finished, work began on a companion, the Alcazar, which was completed in 1889. At the same time, Flagler bought the railroad that connected St. Augustine with Jacksonville

▲ THE BREAKERS' COURTYARD WAS DESIGNED TO RESEMBLE THE GARDENS OF THE VILLA SANTE IN ROME.

◀ THE BREAKERS OPENED IN 1926. THIS SHOT FROM THE GOLF COURSE SHOWS THE HOTEL'S FAMOUS TWIN BELVEDERE TOWERS.

and began to expand it in every direction, linking sleepy resort towns all over Florida. Flagler had begun to build his empire.

NEXT, THE FORMER OIL MAGNATE turned his attention to the town of Palm Beach, about 65 miles north of Miami. In 1894, he built the massive Royal Poinciana Hotel, which dwarfed even his large St. Augustine hostelries. A year later, another hotel, the Palm Beach Inn, southern Florida's first oceanfront resort, was completed. It was enlarged and renamed the Breakers in 1901. Unlike his St. Augustine buildings, Flagler's Palm Beach hotels were made of wood, which, as it turned out, was not his most sound business decision. In 1903, a fire destroyed the Palm Beach Inn. Undaunted, Flagler commissioned a replacement on the same spot. The Breakers II, the second of three hotels that would bear that name, opened less than a year later.

Flagler died in 1913, leaving his descendents and heirs houses, hotels, real estate, artwork, and other investments that they would enjoy for many years. Of his many successful business ventures, however, Flagler was probably most proud of his Florida hotels and railroads. He believed that he had almost single-handedly turned Florida from an uncivilized swamp into a thriving vacation land.

Twelve years after Flagler's death, the second Breakers burned to the ground. Flagler's descendents still owned the property, and they decided to build yet another hotel on the site that Flagler had first chosen for the Palm Beach Inn. This hotel would be more impressive than its two predecessors, a

◀ THROUGHOUT THE HOTEL, THE CORRIDORS ARE STYLISHLY APPOINTED, PROVIDING COMFORTABLE SETTINGS FOR COCKTAILS OR AFTERNOON TEA.

▶ HENRY MORRISON FLAGLER, CIRCA 1909. THE OIL MAGNATE BUILT THE FIRST TWO HOTELS THAT STOOD ON THE BREAKERS' GROUNDS. THE CURRENT STRUCTURE WAS COMPLETED BY HIS HEIRS.

fitting tribute to the man who had practically invented the Florida vacation.

Design and construction of the third hotel to be named the Breakers began immediately. Leonard Schultze, the New York architect who had designed the Waldorf-Astoria Hotel in Manhattan, patterned the new Breakers after the magnificent villas of the Italian Renaissance. His specific model was the famous Villa Medici in Florence. To protect this new hotel from the fate of its predecessors, Schultze chose reinforced steel girders and hollow tile walls as his main construction materials. Work was completed in less than a year, and the hotel opened its doors to guests on December 29, 1926.

T HE HOTEL'S LARGE NINE-
STORY CENTRAL SECTION, facing the street, is topped by twin Belvedere towers which dominate the Palm Beach skyline. North and south wings extend eastward toward the beach, forming a central courtyard that resembles the inner gardens of the Villa Sante in Rome. Graceful archways adorn the front of the hotel, and a magnificent fountain, modeled after the one in Florence's

◄ AS THIS EXAMPLE SUGGESTS, THE FURNISHINGS IN THE GUEST ROOMS ARE SIMPLER IN STYLE THAN THOSE OF THE PUBLIC ROOMS, CREATING A COZY AND HOMEY ATMOSPHERE.

► THE ELEGANT FLORENTINE DINING ROOM FEATURES MAGNIFICENT CHANDELIERS AND A BEAMED CEILING MODELED AFTER THAT WHICH IS IN THE FLORENTINE PALACE DAVANZATE.

Boboli Gardens, guards the entranceway.

The main lobby of the Breakers is splendidly decorated. Its vaulted ceilings, adorned with frescos, and its lavish furnishings recall the artistry of the Italian Renaissance. Bordering the courtyard is the Mediterranean Ballroom. Along with the Venetian Ballroom which faces the ocean, this sumptuous room is the setting for elegant balls and parties. Perhaps the hotel's most impressive gallery is the Gold Room, with its great stone fireplace, its portraits of

explorers who discovered the New World, and its gold-leaf ceiling, a duplicate of that which adorns the Gallerìa Accadèmia in Venice. The Breakers also houses formal dining rooms, meeting rooms, and an arcade of shops.

The Breakers' first guests were 1920s bobbed-haired flappers and their dashing escorts, pulled from the pages of an F. Scott Fitzgerald novel, who came to Palm Beach to frolic on its sandy beaches and partake of its exciting night life. Today's patrons lodge at the hotel for similar reasons. They are also attracted

by the superb recreational facilities available to the Breakers' guests: two golf courses, 20 tennis courts, an Olympic-size heated swimming pool, and a state-of-the-art health club.

During the last two decades, the Breakers has undergone a careful program of expansion and renovation. In 1969, two oceanfront wings were added, expanding the hotel to include 528 guest rooms, 36 suites, and four presidential suites. In 1987, an ambitious five-year, $50 million improvement plan was launched to upgrade and modernize the guest rooms, meeting rooms, kitchen, and resort amenities.

Today the Breakers is owned by the Flagler System, the company formed by Henry Flagler's heirs. Indeed, if Florida's first great hotel tycoon were to look at the edifice created in his honor, he would surely smile in approval.

◀ GUESTS OF THE BREAKERS ENJOY THE AFTERNOON SUN DURING THE LATE 1920S.

▶ THE POOLSIDE LOUNGES OFFER A BREATHTAKING VIEW OF THE ATLANTIC OCEAN.

The Seelbach Hotel
Louisville, Kentucky

· · ·

THE SEELBACH HOTEL in Louisville, Kentucky, is a tribute to the spirit and drive of two German immigrants, Louis and Otto Seelbach. Louis came to America in 1869, at age 17, and settled in Louisville's large German enclave. He took a job at Galt House, the city's grandest hotel, and learned the hotel business. Five years later, Louis began his own version of the American Dream by opening Seelbach's Restaurant and Café on Main Street. In 1880, after several years of hard work, he moved his business to a larger building a few blocks away. Profits were greater in the bigger restaurant; and after five years, Louis was again ready to expand. He summoned his younger brother Otto from Germany, and the two brothers formed the Seelbach Hotel Company. Starting with 30 rooms above their restaurant, they launched their long careers as hoteliers.

The Seelbachs were soon running one of the best hotel-restaurants in Louisville. They used their profits to expand and redecorate, but their vision was bigger still. To realize their dreams,

▲ COLORFUL TILES ADORN THE WALLS OF THE SEELBACH'S GRAND BALLROOM.

◄ THE SEELBACH HOTEL, WHICH OPENED IN 1905, IS A LASTING TRIBUTE TO THE TWO HARD-WORKING GERMAN IMMIGRANTS WHO BUILT IT AND THE TWO DETERMINED LOUISVILLE PRESERVATIONISTS WHO SAVED IT FROM THE WRECKER'S BALL.

they purchased a piece of land on the outskirts of town and, in 1902, began drawing plans for a large luxury hotel that would be Louisville's finest, better

appointed even than the Galt House. They hired architects W. J. Dodd of Louisville and F. M. Andrews of Dayton, Ohio, to make their dream a reality and obtained financing through local bankers, who believed that any enterprise conducted by the two hard-working German immigrants would be worth backing.

Construction began in December 1903. On May 1, 1905, just before the annual running of the Kentucky Derby at nearby Churchill Downs, the Seelbach Hotel opened. More than 25,000 people jammed the lobby and public rooms on opening day to inspect the city's new hostelry. Fifteen hundred guests, including the governor and Louisville's most prominent citizens, attended a formal opening dinner that evening.

The Seelbach's first visitors saw a magnificent ten-story building created in the fashionable turn-of-the-century

Beaux Arts style. The structure was brick with stone trimming and ornate cornices, and it surrounded a large, stylishly landscaped courtyard. The decor and furnishings were luxuriant. The lobby was marble, accented with mahogany and bronze trim, and against one wall stood a stunning fountain made of Rookwood pottery. The main dining room, decorated in the style of the Venetian Renaissance, featured hand-painted friezes, while the hotel bar and Gentlemen's Café were tastefully appointed with hardwood trim and rich furnishings. The second-floor private dining halls were equally impressive, featuring award-winning paintings, plush Persian carpeting, and fine leather furniture. Brass and costly hardwood beds distinguished the 196 guest rooms. For guests seeking a panoramic view of Louisville and the Ohio River, the Seelbachs thoughtfully provided a tenth-floor roof garden. Moreover, the new hotel was equipped with all the turn-of-the-century conveniences— electric chandeliers, long-distance telephone booths, and private baths.

T HE HOTEL was an immediate success. The Seelbachs soon planned an addition—a wing that would house more guest rooms, a first-floor German Rathskeller, and an enclosed rooftop ballroom with a hardwood dance floor. The Rathskeller's floors, walls, and columns were made of rare Rookwood pottery, and its ceiling was covered with leather. The room was

DURING THE LATE 1970S, EACH ROOM AND SUITE IN THE SEELBACH WAS COMPLETELY RESTORED. PICTURED HERE IS THE ELEGANT PRESIDENTIAL SUITE.

THE OLD
SEELBACH BAR
IS A POPULAR
GATHERING
PLACE FOR
LOUISVILLE'S
SOCIALITES.
THE CHAIRS AND
STOOLS ARE
TRIMMED WITH
HANDSOME
LEATHER.

also air-conditioned, one of the first rooms in America to feature this modern convenience.

The Seelbach attracted not only Louisville's most prominent citizens but also celebrities and dignitaries from around the United States. During the 1920s, the hotel became the setting for rousing Jazz Age parties and receptions. F. Scott Fitzgerald even used the Seelbach—under the pseudonym "the Mulbach"—as the locus for the wedding of Daisy Buchanan, the Louisville debutante in *The Great Gatsby*. Presidents William Taft and Woodrow Wilson were the first to stay at the Seelbach. In subsequent years, Franklin Roosevelt, Harry Truman, John Kennedy, and Lyndon Johnson also rented rooms and suites.

Louis Seelbach died in 1925, and Otto died eight years later. Subsequent owners substantially remodeled their hotel. Rooms were rearranged, wall murals were covered with plaster, and the Rathskeller was made into a theater. But the hotel continued to turn a profit for another 35 years after Otto's death. During the late 1960s, however, Louisville experienced many of the problems that plagued other American cities— urban decay, crime, the flight to the suburbs. On July 1, 1975, after several years of red-ink budgeting, the Seelbach closed its doors. Empty, the old building began to deteriorate.

FORTUNATELY, the Seelbach still stands, for if the hotel was a memorial to two hard-working immigrants, it is also a tribute to two determined Louisville preservationists,

▲ THE PRESIDENTIAL SUITE'S MASTER BEDROOM CONTAINS A HANDSOME FOUR-POSTER BED WITH A BRIGHTLY COLORED QUILT AND FRAMED FOLK ART ON THE WALLS.

◄ THE LOBBY IN THE SEELBACH IS SEEN HERE IN AN UNDATED PERIOD PHOTOGRAPH.

H. G. Whittenberg and Roger Davis, who purchased the unoccupied Seelbach in 1978 and vowed to reopen it as soon as renovation was completed. That process took almost four years and cost $24 million, but in April 1982 the grand hotel reopened its doors.

The Seelbach Hotel now contains 324 splendidly appointed rooms and suites, each furnished with a stylish mahogany four-poster bed. Its lobby has been restored to its turn-of-the-century splendor with marble columns supporting the elegantly

▲ MANY OF THE SEELBACH'S SUITES ARE EQUIPPED WITH FORMAL DINING ROOMS, INCLUDING THE ONE PICTURED HERE.

◀ THE OAK ROOM, NAMED FOR ITS HANDSOME OAK PANELING, OFFERS GOURMET MEALS IN AN ELEGANT SETTING.

THE INTRICATE MOLDING IN THE GOLD MEETING ROOM TESTIFIES TO THE SKILLED CRAFTSMANSHIP OF A BYGONE AGE.

detailed ceiling, and a long staircase with a bronze banister leading to the second floor. Historic murals by Arthur Thomas adorn the lobby walls, and palm plants and floral arrangements enhance the decor.

The dining rooms, meeting rooms, and ballrooms have also been carefully restored. The rooftop ballroom is still the setting for weddings and prestigious events. The elegant Oak Room again offers visitors some of the best gourmet meals in Louisville, and the Café serves breakfast, lunch, and dinner in an informal setting. The Old Seelbach Bar is once again a meeting place for Louisville's socialites, and the Rathskeller, the world's only remaining Rookwood pottery room, has regained its prominent place on the city's social registry.

The restoration of the Seelbach, now owned and operated by Medallion Hotels, helped spark a program of renewal and revitalization in downtown Louisville. The city's citizens and the hotel's guests are certainly pleased that the hard work of the Seelbach brothers, Davis, and Whittenberg was not wasted.

The Grand Hotel
Mackinac Island, Michigan

THE HURON AND IROQUOIS INDIANS considered the small island in the strait between Lake Michigan and Lake Huron a sacred site, the birthplace of Michabou, God of Waters. According to legend, Michabou and other great spirits lived in caves beneath the island and roamed its woods searching for tasty fruits and herbs. To the Native Americans, the island was a paradise on earth, a place where the gods resided and man was a respectful visitor. Because of its shape, the Indians called the island "Michilimackinac," which means Great Turtle.

Today, a first-time visitor to Mackinac Island—the final "c" is pronounced as a "w"— might also believe that he or she had landed in paradise. A narrow beach leads to high grassy bluffs and woodlands. To the east and west are the resplendent waters of the two Great Lakes. To the southwest, one can see the graceful

Mackinac Bridge, connecting Michigan's upper and lower peninsulas. And sitting atop the island's highest hill is a magnificent hotel of impressive proportions and appearance—the Grand Hotel of Mackinac Island.

▲ THE GRAND IS A SLEEK, LOW-LYING STRUCTURE THAT COMPLEMENTS THE HORIZONTAL LINES OF MACKINAC ISLAND'S BLUFFS. IN THE FOREGROUND IS THE HOTEL'S SERPENTINE SWIMMING POOL.

◄ HORSE-DRAWN CARRIAGES LINE THE FRONT ENTRANCE TO THE GRAND HOTEL. THESE VEHICLES ARE THE MOST POPULAR MODE OF TRANSPORTATION ON MACKINAC ISLAND, WHERE MOTORIZED TRANSPORT IS NOT PERMITTED.

The Grand Hotel was conceived by Francis B. Stockbridge, a Michigan businessman and politician who owned a cottage in the Annex, a fashionable

Mackinac vacation community. In 1882, Stockbridge purchased some land on the island and began making plans for a grand luxury lodge on the site to accommodate the growing number of Michigan mainlanders coming to Mackinac to enjoy the island's clean air and breathtaking views. Before he could put his plan into action, however, Stockbridge was elected to the U.S. Senate, so he sold his land to three transportation companies— the Michigan Central Railroad, the Grand Rapids & Indiana Railroad, and the Detroit & Cleveland Steamship Navigation Company. The new owners formed the Mackinac Island Hotel Company and, in 1886, hired Charles Caskey, a well-known resort builder from Harbor Springs, Michigan, to create a grand hotel that would exceed in size and grandeur the island's existing hotels—Island House, Lakeview Hotel, and Mission House.

THE GRAND'S SUITES PROVIDE LUXURIOUS ACCOMMODATIONS FOR SPECIAL MACKINAC ISLAND VACATIONERS. PICTURED HERE IS THE MILLIKEN SUITE.

IN 1979, THE GRAND HOTEL BECAME THE IDYLLIC SETTING FOR *SOMEWHERE IN TIME*, A ROMANTIC FILM STARRING CHRISTOPHER REEVE *(LEFT)*, CHRISTOPHER PLUMMER, AND JANE SEYMOUR.

THE LATE 1880s were a time of architectural ostentation and flamboyance, but Caskey had other ideas for Mackinac's new hotel. He envisioned a sleek, low-lying structure that would complement the horizontal lines of the bluffs on which it would sit. The hotel would be only four stories tall and would be fronted by a classic columned porch long and wide enough to serve as a stately promenade and reception area. Caskey designed a simple roof with two small central Queen Anne gables and a handsome cupola that would be visible from the mainland across the Straits of Mackinac. A crew of 300 laborers and craftsmen completed the building in only three months; and when it was finished in July 1887, Mackinac Island had a handsome new hotel, one that more closely resembled George Washington's stately Mt. Vernon plantation house than the fashionable Victorian seaside resorts of the day.

Throughout the 1890s, the Grand Hotel attracted gentlemen and ladies of wealth and leisure who paid as much as $5.00 per night for lodgings—not including meals. Potter Palmer, the famous Chicago hotelier, was an occasional guest. The beer-making Busch family of St. Louis and the Swift and Armour families of meat-packing fame vacationed at the Grand. Samuel Clemens, the great humorist who wrote under the name Mark Twain, lectured at the hotel. And countless politicians and dignitaries crossed the Straits of Mackinac to spend a summer holiday at the Grand.

The hotel was significantly expanded during its first quarter century. A west wing housing 50 additional rooms was built in 1897. Around 1900, a fifth story was erected. Later a west wing was added. Business declined around 1910 and the hotel's owners considered razing the building, but new ownership saved the hotel. Under the new regime, a swimming pool was built, rooms were remodeled, and plumbing was improved, and by 1920 the Grand was again turning a profit. In 1925, William Stewart Woodfill, originally hired as a summer desk clerk, bought the hotel and ran it for most of the next 50 years. His aggressive promotions and his insistence on quality service ensured the hotel's continued success.

Today, the Grand Hotel is indeed a restful place in an earthly paradise. Vacationers who are troubled by the traffic jams at other summer resorts find

THE TEDDY ROOSEVELT ROOM, NAMED FOR THE AVID HUNTER, SPORTSMAN, AND U.S. PRESIDENT, IS ACCENTED WITH HUNTING TROPHIES.

it splendidly refreshing that automobiles are prohibited on Mackinac Island. The local residents and visitors get about on bicycle, on horseback, in horse-drawn surrey, or on foot. (The island is only 3 miles long and 2 miles wide.) Traffic jams, air pollution, and vehicle noise are not found on Mackinac Island.

THE VENERABLE HOTEL on the bluffs is as majestic as ever. A program of remodeling and restoration begun in the 1980s has both modernized the hotel—fourth-floor rooms were converted to luxury suites—and preserved its century-old heritage. The Grand now contains 317 guest rooms, individually and tastefully decorated. A newly redesigned golf course, the Jewel, borders the hotel, and a serpentine swimming pool, reached by a long stairway and flanked by colorful gardens, lies near the foot of the bluff on which the hotel sits. Tennis courts, jogging paths, and an exercise course enable guests to follow as strenuous a physical regimen as they like during their stay. A new conference center caters to business executives, and a theater offers feature films.

The hotel's public rooms are perhaps its most appealing feature. The cozy parlor just inside the main entrance is filled with comfortable Victorian-style furniture and decorated with tasteful antiques, creating the perfect environment for high tea, which is served every afternoon. Salle à Manger, the main dining room, provides an elegant setting for breakfast, lunch, or dinner. Two lounges offer afternoon and

◀ NO MACKINAC ISLAND VACATION IS COMPLETE WITHOUT A DINNER IN SALLE À MANGER, THE GRAND'S FORMAL DINING HALL.

▶ THE GALLERY OF THE GRAND HOTEL IS ELEGANTLY APPOINTED WITH SOFT SOFAS AND EASY CHAIRS, A BRIGHTLY PATTERNED CARPET, AND A SPARKLING CHANDELIER. GREEN IS THE COLOR THAT ONE FINDS IN MOST OF THE HOTEL'S PUBLIC ROOMS.

evening cocktails, and Carleton's Tea Store serves light lunches and ice cream.

The most popular public area is the 880-foot covered front porch. Furnished with rocking chairs and bordered by colorful flower boxes, this splendid veranda provides a panoramic view of Lake Huron. The porch is the Grand Hotel's most distinctive feature and is enjoyed by guests at all hours of the day.

Visitors to the Grand Hotel, which is now owned by the Musser family, can also enjoy the other attractions of Mackinac Island, including Fort Mackinac, Mission Church, and dozens of colonial cabins and 19th-century Victorian homes.

THE GRAND'S MOST POPULAR PUBLIC AREA IS ITS 880-FOOT COVERED FRONT PORCH, WHICH OFFERS A SPLENDID VIEW OF LAKE HURON.

The Drake

The Drake Hotel
Chicago, Illinois

THE DRAKE HOTEL is a lasting tribute to the vision of Ben Marshall, a Chicago architect, and John and Tracy Drake, the sons of John Burroughs Drake, one of the Windy City's great 19th-century hoteliers. The elder John Drake, an Ohio native who had left home as a teenager to take a hotel job in Cincinnati, arrived in Chicago in 1855 and bought a share of the old Tremont House. According to legend, Drake became one of the captains of the Chicago hotel industry during the Great Chicago Fire of 1871. After watching the Tremont House burn to the ground, he walked to Michigan Avenue where the fire was consuming buildings. There he saw the great Michigan Avenue Hotel's worried proprietor pacing the street and offered to buy the building and all its furnishings on the spot. The hotel's owner thought Drake

crazy, but he signed over his investment immediately at a fire-sale price.

Drake's purchase turned out to be a worthwhile gamble, because the fire stopped just short of his new hotel.

▲ THE PALM COURT ON THE UPPER LOBBY HAS AS ITS CENTERPIECE A 260-YEAR-OLD FRENCH BRONZE URN FILLED WITH FLOWERS AND SET IN A HANDSOME MARBLE FOUNTAIN.

◀ THE DRAKE, A 13-STORY, 700-ROOM HOTEL BUILT IN THE STYLE OF THE ITALIAN RENAISSANCE, OPENED IN 1920.

Afterwards, Drake had title to one of Chicago's few remaining lodging places. Not only did he make a fortune, he also became one of the most famous hotel-

keepers in the country, competing for many years with Potter Palmer, another wealthy Chicago hotelier who built and twice rebuilt the Palmer House.

Drake's sons followed their father's career path, but it was Marshall, the architect, who suggested building the hotel that would carry their family name. Convinced that Chicago's Near North Side would one day be the center of the city's business district, he became particularly interested in a piece of real estate at the northern end of Michigan Avenue, an area that had once been part of Lake Michigan but had been landfilled and was awaiting development. Marshall imagined a grand hotel rising on the site, one that would overlook spectacular Lake Michigan and Oak Street Beach and would serve well-to-do tourists and businessmen who visited Chicago. In 1917, the Drakes agreed to finance Marshall's idea. Their

IN 1921, WHEN THIS PICTURE WAS TAKEN, VISITORS TOOK TO THE BEACH BEHIND THE DRAKE HOTEL JUST AS THEY DO TODAY, ALTHOUGH THEY WORE A GOOD DEAL MORE CLOTHING DURING THE ROARING TWENTIES.

new creation would be a splendid lodge that even would surpass in beauty and luxury the great hotels that John Drake, Sr., had owned.

INSPIRED BY THE GREAT PALACES of Rome and Florence, Marshall designed a 13-story, 700-room hotel in the style of the Italian Renaissance. For the building's walls, he used solid Bedford limestone; for the floors, he chose Tennessee marble. Marshall began with a rectangular base and shifted at the third story to an H-shape, a pattern that allowed a large number of the hotel's guest rooms to have a view of Lake Michigan. The Drake Hotel cost some $10 million; but when it opened on New Year's Eve in 1920, Chicago had a grand new lodging place, according to an article in *The Economist,* "of unusual magnificence, nothing like it in appear-

ance, arrangement or finishing having ever been attempted in this country."

The Drake Hotel, with its stunning double-level lobby and its lavish guest rooms, quickly became one of Chicago's finest stopovers. A stream of celebrities—President Herbert Hoover, Bing Crosby, Katharine Hepburn, Sinclair Lewis, Walt Disney—passed through its doors. It was continually renovated and modernized to compete with the new hotels that arose with Chicago's increasing importance as a business center. In 1933, however, the Drake family, suffering from losses during the Great Depression, sold the hotel to Edward L. Brashears, who had married Marshall's niece. During World War II, the Drake was leased to the U.S. Government as military lodging; but after the war ended, it was redecorated and opened again as a grand hotel.

In the years since World War II, Chicago's North Side has changed a great deal. Today, the Drake sits at the head of Chicago's "Magnificent Mile," the string of office buildings, galleries, theaters, shops, and restaurants along Michigan Avenue. Just a few steps from the hotel's doors is the 95-story John Hancock Center. Nearby are Water Tower Place, the 110-story Sears Tower, and a dozen other buildings that make the Drake appear like a small child standing among taller siblings.

But the Drake is more handsome than ever. The hotel's original 700 rooms have been converted to 535 guest rooms; 66 suites, including a Presidential Suite; four major banquet rooms; 14 smaller meeting rooms; and two luxury boardrooms. A $20 million renovation project completed in 1986, supervised by David T. Williams, has turned Ben

THE GOLD COAST
ROOM IS THE
DRAKE'S MOST
IMPRESSIVE
BANQUET HALL.
DESIGNED IN
THE STYLE OF
THE ITALIAN
RENAISSANCE,
IT FEATURES
GOLD- AND
CREAM-COLORED
COLUMNS,
MARBLE FLOORS,
AND CRYSTAL
CHANDELIERS.

◀ THE COZY
CAPE COD ROOM
HAS EARNED A
REPUTATION
AS ONE OF
CHICAGO'S
FINEST SEAFOOD
RESTAURANTS.

▶ THE DRAKE'S
SPECTACULAR
TWO-LEVEL
LOBBY IS
BEDECKED WITH
RICH ORIENTAL
CARPETS,
SPARKLING
CHANDELIERS,
AND TASTEFUL
FURNISHINGS.

Marshall's creation into an international hotel of the finest order.

WILLIAMS BEGAN HIS WORK by redesigning the Drake's lobbies. Today's guests enter a stately room carpeted with rich Oriental rugs and lit by an impressive chandelier hanging from the ornately detailed ceiling. A wide stairway leads to the upper lobby, called "the Palm Court," which has as its centerpiece a 260-year-old French bronze urn, filled with fresh flowers and set in a marble fountain. Hanging plants, indoor palms, and floral-print couches help create a relaxing and cozy atmosphere—the perfect setting for afternoon tea or cocktails.

Williams also redecorated the Gold Coast Room, the Drake's most impressive banquet hall. It is designed in Italian Renaissance style, with gold- and cream-colored columns, marble floors, and large crystal chandeliers. The Grand Ballroom, which is Georgian in decor, features a hardwood floor and beautifully crafted sconces on the walls.

THE MASTER BEDROOM OF THE PRESIDENTIAL SUITE PROVIDES ITS OCCUPANTS WITH A SWEEPING VIEW OF LAKE MICHIGAN AND LAKE SHORE DRIVE.

◄ FRESH FLORAL ARRANGEMENTS ADD COLOR TO THE DRAKE'S INVITING LOBBY.

Another banquet room, the French Room, is appointed with furnishings and artwork of the period of Louis XVI, and the Drake's private Club International is a replica of Haddon Hall, an English mansion in Derbyshire. The varied styles of these rooms add to the charm of the Drake's public areas. In addition to the Club International, the Drake houses three other restaurants—the Cape Cod Room, one of Chicago's best seafood eateries;

Coq d'Or, a lounge serving lunch and late-night supper; and the Oak Terrace Room, with its splendid view of Lake Michigan. A new shopping arcade was added in 1984.

The Drake, on the National Register of Historic Places since 1981, is now operated by Hilton International Company. Its staff of 650 is dedicated to the same goal that inspired the Drake brothers seven decades ago—providing luxury accommodations for visitors to the Windy City.

THE PRESIDENTIAL SUITE HOUSES ANTIQUES AND OBJETS D'ART, LIKE THIS RECLINING CHERUB AND DOG SET ON A MARBLE FIREPLACE MANTLE.

The Brown Palace Hotel
Denver, Colorado

• • •

DURING THE CENTURY since the Brown Palace Hotel opened its doors, the city of Denver has changed from a cattle and mining town to a bustling American metropolis. Large glass-and-steel buildings now dwarf the grand hotel that once dominated the Mile High City skyline. Government offices, museums and theaters, and the handsome 16th Street Pedestrian Mall surround the triangle of land on 17th Street and Broadway in downtown Denver where the Palace majestically stands. A professional urban population, drawn to the city by the aerospace and high-tech industries that developed in the 1960s, and Yuppie vacationers, who visit Denver en route to Colorado's famous ski resorts, have kept the city alive and vibrant a century and a half after the cattlemen and miners first settled the Colorado Territories.

In this contemporary urban setting, the Brown Palace Hotel stands as a monument to Denver's past. Its rich Italian Renaissance design and its Victorian

▲ ELABORATE IRON RAILINGS SERVE AS BALCONIES FOR THE HOTEL'S UPPER FLOORS. THE LIGHTED ARCHWAYS PROVIDE A GRAND VIEW OF THE LOBBY BELOW.

◄ THE BROWN PALACE HOTEL, WHICH OPENED IN 1892, OCCUPIES A TRIANGULAR PIECE OF LAND AT 17TH AND TREMONT STREETS IN DOWNTOWN DENVER.

flavor recall the late 19th century, when Denver was establishing itself as a commercial center for businessmen whose products crossed the American continent. The Brown Palace, triangular in shape

and nine stories high, vividly calls to mind the aura of an earlier century, when Victorian ladies and gentlemen first brought culture and civilization to the land shadowed by the Rocky Mountains.

The front doors of the Brown Palace open to an atrium lobby, eight stories high and topped by a stained-glass ceiling of 2,800 square feet. The lobby walls are made of gold onyx, and the floors are white marble. Guests lounging in the lobby's oxblood-colored leather couches and easy chairs can gaze upward and admire the six tiers of elaborate cast iron railings that serve as balconies for the upper floors, which house 230 guest rooms, 12 meeting rooms, and 25 luxury suites. The suites, located on the eighth and ninth floors, are faced with glass brick, giving the atrium's top levels an art deco look.

Each of the Palace's guest rooms is individual in style and appointment, from elegant Victorian to art deco, and all of the rooms have windows that provide occupants with a view of downtown Denver. In the hotel's early days, patrons were asked if they preferred the morning or afternoon sun, and they were provided with a room on the appropriate side of the building.

The Brown Palace also houses award-winning restaurants and lounges. The Palace Arms, the hotel's formal dining room, is decorated in Napoleonic style, with French military prints adorning the walls and Napoleonic memorabilia prominently displayed. Ellyngton's, the hotel's main dining room, offers breakfast, lunch, and Sunday brunch. The Ship Tavern, with its authentic nautical furnishings and impressive collection of model clipper ships, serves Rocky Mountain trout and other seafood delights. Henry C's lounge provides guests with the opportunity to relax over cocktails. The lobby maintains the British tradition of afternoon tea, served on tables patterned after those found in Vienna coffeehouses.

▶ THE PRESIDENTIAL SUITE, SHOWN HERE, IS NAMED FOR DWIGHT D. EISENHOWER. IN 1952, "IKE" USED THE BROWN PALACE AS HIS PRE-CONVENTION HEADQUARTERS.

▼ PRESIDENT EISENHOWER RETURNED TO THE BROWN PALACE FOR AN AMERICAN LEGION CHRISTMAS PARTY FOR CHILDREN.

THIS GRAND HOTEL was created by Henry C. Brown, an Ohio builder who arrived in Denver with his wife and child in an ox cart in 1860. He had reportedly made a fortune working in San Francisco in the 1850s

▲ HENRY C. BROWN, FOUNDER OF THE BROWN PALACE HOTEL.

◄ THE SHIP'S TAVERN RESTAURANT HOLDS AN IMPRESSIVE COLLECTION OF MODEL CLIPPER SHIPS AND OTHER SAILING MEMORABILIA. PATRONS CAN ENJOY ROCKY MOUNTAIN TROUT AND OTHER SEAOOD SPECIALTIES.

and had promptly lost his money on a hotel in Decatur, Nebraska, when that town failed to turn into the thriving metropolis that Brown had imagined it would become. In Denver, he again made money as a builder and, for a time, operated the *Denver Tribune*. His interests spread to banking, real estate, and the railroads; and, by the late 1880s, he was again a wealthy man. About that time, he acquired the triangle of land on 17th Street and Broadway and commissioned Frank E. Edbrooke, a Chicago architect who had moved to Denver, to design his hotel.

The contracting firm of Geddes and Seerie used granite from the Rocky Mountains, sandstone from Arizona,

► THE BROWN PALACE'S NINE-STORY ATRIUM LOBBY HAS GOLD ONYX WALLS, WHITE MARBLE FLOORS, AND HANDSOME VICTORIAN FURNISHINGS.

THE INDEPENDENCE ROOM, PICTURED HERE, IS ONE OF THE BROWN PALACE'S 12
MEETING ROOMS, USED FOR BANQUETS AND RECEPTIONS.

and onyx from Mexico to implement Edbrooke's design. Only stone and steel were used in erecting the building, ensuring that Brown's investment would never go up in fire and smoke. Builders dug two 700-feet artesian wells to supply the hotel with water. State-of-the-art heating, plumbing, and electrical equipment was used. The hotel cost $1.6 million to build, with another $400,000 spent on furnishings. In August 1892, the Brown Palace received its first guests. The price of a room ranged from $1.00 to $4.50 per night.

Brown almost lost his hotel and his fortune during the Silver Panic of 1893, which financially devastated Denver. But through the difficult 1890s, the Brown Palace continued to attract guests and began to build a national reputation. Brown was forced to mortgage his hotel to cover some of his sour investments, but he retained part ownership in the Palace until he died in 1906 at age 86.

SINCE BROWN'S DEATH, ownership of the hotel has changed hands several times and the Palace has been periodically emended and updated. For example, the large fireplace that once warmed the lobby now serves as an entranceway to the retail shops on the first floor. Fireplaces have been removed from the guest rooms, and air conditioning has been added. The top-floor ballroom was made into suites; and, in 1959, the Brown Palace Tower, housing additional guest rooms, was built across the way on Tremont Street. Today it is a separate hotel.

OXBLOOD LEATHER EASY CHAIRS AND SOFAS ARE PLACED THROUGHOUT THE HOTEL'S PUBLIC ROOMS. THIS CHAIR IS SET IN THE SITTING ROOM NEAR THE SHIP'S TAVERN RESTAURANT.

Over the years, Brown's hotel has served a number of prominent patrons. At the turn of the century, Denver's "Unsinkable" Molly Brown—no relation to Henry Brown—was a frequent visitor. President Teddy Roosevelt spoke at a banquet at the Palace in 1905. Woodrow Wilson, Herbert Hoover, and Franklin D. Roosevelt slept there; and, in 1952, Dwight D. Eisenhower used the hotel as his preconvention headquarters. But perhaps the Palace's most famous guests were four rock stars from Liverpool. When word got out that the Beatles were staying at the hotel during their 1964 Denver engagement, Broadway and 17th Street swarmed with screaming teenagers anxious to get a glimpse of their new idols.

Today the Brown Palace is owned by Integrated Resources, Inc., and managed by Rank Hotels North America. Guests, whether they are presidents, rock stars, vacationers, or business executives, are catered to by staff members who undergo a special hospitality course stressing friendly and efficient service, part of an effort to ensure that the patrons of the Palace today enjoy the splendor of Denver's past and the comforts of the 20th century.

The Old Faithful Inn
Yellowstone National Park, Wyoming

• • •

MANY OF THE GRAND HOTELS built during the last two decades of the 19th century—the Waldorf in New York, the Brown Palace in Denver, the Hotel del Coronado in Coronado, California—were designed as monuments to their makers, magnificent Beaux Arts and Victorian creations which stand out from their surrounding landscapes and demand attention. Robert C. Reamer, a young Ohio-born architect, used an entirely different approach when, in 1902, he was asked by the Yellowstone Park Association to design a lodge near Old Faithful Geyser in Yellowstone Park, Wyoming. Reamer's creation, the Old Faithful Inn, stands as a splendid example of a building that exists in harmony with its environment.

By the turn of the century, Yellowstone Park was already drawing thousands of affluent visitors. For those who did not wish to camp out, however, the available accommodations were terrible. The Fountain Hotel, a fashionable lodge that was a rugged 10-mile ride from Old Faithful, and the Shack Hotel, a canvas-covered struc-

▲ FOR THE INN'S LOBBY, ARCHITECT ROBERT REAMER USED MATERIALS INDIGENOUS TO THE REGION—LARGE TREE TRUNKS, PINE LOGS, AND TWISTED LODGEPOLES.

◄ THE OLD FAITHFUL INN, DESIGNED BY OHIO-BORN ROBERT C. REAMER, OPENED ITS DOORS TO YELLOWSTONE PARK LODGERS IN 1904. TODAY IT IS OWNED BY THE NATIONAL PARK SERVICE.

ture that was really a tent, were the only lodging places in the area. So in the summer of 1903, work began on Reamer's hotel.

Reamer certainly imagined a grand hotel—but one that would complement the area's scenic natural landscape. For his main construction materials, he chose what Yellowstone Park offered: volcanic rock, stones of all sizes, high pine trees, and twisted lodgepole tree limbs. He built his inn's foundation with rhyolite, the same volcanic rock that lines the ridge behind Old Faithful. On the first story, he topped the rhyolite with long pines, creating a log cabin look. Supplementing the area's resources, he imported red-painted cedar shingles from California to cover the upper stories, and glass, plumbing, and heating equipment. But much of the hotel's hardware—door hinges, ceiling lamps—was forged at the worksite.

When construction was complete, Reamer's inn, which rose seven stories, featured a large central block with a steeply slanted roof, dotted randomly with windowed dormers, and two wings with large front gables. The entire building was 300 feet long and 79 feet high at the rooftop porch. At a time when large hotels, even those made of wood, had budgets of several million dollars, Reamer's creation cost a modest $140,000.

THE OLD FAITHFUL INN opened in the spring of 1904. Its first guests pulled up to its covered porte cochere in stagecoaches and on horseback and entered the inn through huge split-log double doors. The lobby, 76 feet high, resembled an oversized log cabin. The walls were made of long logs held in place by vertical tree-like columns. The stairways leading to the upstairs rooms were constructed with hand-hewn split pine logs. And the open balconies on the upper floors were trimmed with railings made of twisted lodgepoles.

But this rugged-looking lodge had many of the comforts that turn-of-the-century travelers demanded. The lobby's wood-plank floors were covered with patterned wool carpets. Comfortable easy chairs and rockers beckoned guests to relax as they would in the public rooms of a grand metropolitan hotel. In the center of the lobby stood a giant lavastone fireplace, 40 feet high. A clock forged on the site (and still in use) was set on the mantel, high above the hearth. The large dining room featured colorful draperies, immaculate white table cloths, and fine dishes and utensils, and guests were expected to dress formally for dinner. During the evening, orchestras entertained patrons with chamber music in the lobby. The inn's 140 rustic guest rooms also offered desirable amenities—four-poster iron beds, frilled curtains, comfortable chairs.

Since its opening, the Old Faithful Inn has undergone many changes. Two flat-roofed wings, one built in 1913 and the other in 1927, have been added to the original inn, making it 800 feet long and giving it approximately 350 guest rooms. In 1927, the lobby was expanded outward. The porte cochere was pushed forward and topped with an open-air deck, and the original stageway in front of the inn was replaced with a concrete walkway. In 1940, the logs in the lobby were stripped of their bark; and, in 1966,

PICTURED HERE IS THE FIRST AUTO TO GO THROUGH YELLOWSTONE NATIONAL PARK. THE PHOTO WAS TAKEN BEFORE THE OLD FAITHFUL INN IN 1915.

THE LOBBY
FIREPLACE,
40 FEET HIGH,
IS BUILT WITH
GIANT
LAVASTONES
GATHERED
FROM THE
SURROUNDING
REGION.

ETCHED GLASS
WINDOWS ADD A
TOUCH OF
ELEGANCE TO
THE INN'S
FORMAL
DINING ROOM.

they were covered with varnish to prevent decay.

RENOVATION IS A CONTINUING TASK. During the past few years, the inn's shingle siding and roof have been replaced, the dining room chimney has been rebuilt, and a new fire protection system has been installed. The need to modernize and renovate has always been balanced with the need to preserve the inn's original frontier character.

Though the access roads have improved and other more modern lodging places have been built, Yellowstone National Park still looks as it did when the inn was built. Old Faithful still gushes forth its steam and boiling water at predictable intervals. The 3,472-square-mile park, which since 1916 has been administered by the National Park Service, is still home to bear, elk, bighorn sheep, deer, bison, coyote, and numerous other species of wildlife. Hot bubbling pools and colorful paint pots still dominate the area, revealing geological secrets millions of years old. Yellowstone Lake, home to fish and waterfowl, still empties into the Yellowstone River with its spectacular waterfall. Moose still cool themselves in the shallows along the lake's 110-mile shoreline.

Yellowstone's visitors are still nature lovers who relish the chance to

THE INN'S INDIVIDUAL GUEST ROOMS OFFER SIMPLE BUT TASTEFUL, COMFORTABLE FURNISHINGS IN A RUSTIC SETTING.

cover the park on foot, horseback, snowshoes, and cross-country skis. In this splendidly pristine setting, the Old Faithful Inn, which was designated a National Historical Landmark in 1987 and is now owned by the National Park Service, stands as a symbol, an architectural creation that reflects the grandeur of its surroundings. It offers its guests the comfort of home without drawing undue attention from the beauties of the natural landscape in which it stands.

THE GEYSER OLD FAITHFUL STILL ERUPTS AT PREDICTABLE INTERVALS. THE INN CAN BE SEEN IN THE BACKGROUND.

The Arizona Biltmore
Phoenix, Arizona

◆ ◆ ◆

IN *AN AUTOBIOGRAPHY*, Frank Lloyd Wright, the great American architect, claimed that "No house should ever be *on* any hill or on anything. It should be *of* the hill, belonging to it, so the hill and house could live together each the happier for the other." Encapsulated in this statement is the essence of Wright's theory of "Organic Architecture." A building should complement the natural landscape on which it sits; it should be composed of indigenous construction materials blended in such a way that the building and its environment form a unified, organic whole. The ultimate expression of this theory is Fallingwater, the home designed by Wright for Edgar J. Kaufmann in Mill Run, Pennsylvania, that appears to be naturally related to the stream and waterfall along which it sits.

The design of the Arizona Bilt-more in Phoenix is not officially credited to Frank Lloyd Wright. The architect listed on the hotel's blueprints is Albert Chase McArthur, a former Wright apprentice who had worked in the mas-

▲ BILTMORE PATRONS CAN QUENCH THEIR THIRST IN THE LOGGIA, A BAR LOCATED IN THE HOTEL LOBBY.

◀ THE ARIZONA BILTMORE, WHICH OPENED IN 1929, IS AN EXCELLENT EXAMPLE OF FRANK LLOYD WRIGHT'S THEORY OF "ORGANIC ARCHITECTURE."

ter's Oak Park, Illinois, studio in 1909. Eighteen years later, when his two brothers bought a piece of land in Phoenix and began to plan a lavish hotel and resort complex, McArthur contacted his old mentor and asked for assistance. Wright, who had five years earlier completed the famous Imperial Hotel in Tokyo, jumped at the chance to employ his theory of Organic Architecture to the Arizona desert. So he signed on as a consultant, and the two men began to plan the new hotel.

Even today, architectural critics and Wright biographers disagree on how much of the Arizona Biltmore is Wright's and how much is McArthur's. Some say that the master "ghost"-designed the building while his former student was given credit. McArthur maintained that the work was his own, and Wright defended that claim in a statement published in *The Architectural Record*. Regardless of how much each architect contributed to the final plans, the Arizona Biltmore bears many of the trademarks of a Wright creation.

SAGUARO FORMS AND CACTUS FLOWERS, A STAINED GLASS MURAL DESIGNED BY FRANK LLOYD WRIGHT, IS FEATURED IN THE BILTMORE'S LOBBY.

THE INFLUENCE OF FRANK LLOYD WRIGHT, ONE OF AMERICA'S MOST CELEBRATED ARCHITECTS, CAN BE FELT THROUGHOUT THE ARIZONA BILTMORE.

The Biltmore, which opened in February 1929, is constructed of large precast concrete blocks, a building system that Wright invented and used in several Los Angeles homes that he built in the early 1920s. The patterned blocks were molded at the work site with Arizona desert sand, under Wright's supervision. The other essential building materials—copper for the roof and gold for the gold-leaf ceilings—are also

indigenous to the surrounding area. Like many other Wright buildings, the Arizona Biltmore is built low to the ground—four stories tall, and Wright supposedly preferred only three—and is asymmetrical in shape with varying levels. Viewed from afar, the hotel appears as a sandy mesa rising naturally from the surrounding desertscape.

The hotel's interiors also carry the stamp of Frank Lloyd Wright. In the Biltmore's foyer is a mini-oasis, a cluster of columns and plants. The lobby is long, with an overhanging mezzanine that blurs the division between levels. Wright-designed furniture and carpeting and Wright's artworks are used throughout the public rooms. Perhaps the most distinctive of these is the back-lit, geometric, stained glass mural entitled *Saguaro Forms and Cactus Flowers,*

THE CAFÉ SONORA OFFERS SOUTH-OF-THE-BORDER SPECIALTIES IN AN INFORMAL ATMOSPHERE.

which is set in the hotel's foyer. Curtains, carpets, furniture, and wall hangings in many of the guest rooms were also reproduced from Wright's designs. Moreover, six sculptures—Biltmore Sprites created by Wright and sculptor Alfonso Ianelli in 1914—have recently been placed on the hotel grounds.

Like other Wright creations, the Arizona Biltmore also contains rooms of various geometric shapes. The one which draws the most attention is the octagon-shaped Aztec Room, which was formerly the Aztec Lounge. (Wright's first studio in Oak Park also contained an octagonal room.) This impressive space has a majestic domed ceiling covered in gold leaf, copper-accented supporting beams, and a sunken cocktail bar with an inlaid brass top.

TODAY'S ARIZONA BILTMORE is much larger than the original hotel and cottages on which Wright worked. From 1929, when William Wrigley, Jr., the Chicago chewing gum tycoon, bought the hotel, until 1973, when the Wrigley family sold the complex to Talley Industries, only one major addition—a grand ballroom—was created. Under Talley ownership, however, the Biltmore was greatly expanded to meet Arizona's growing number of winter vacationers. In 1975, the 90-room Paradise Wing was built. In 1979,

◄ THE BILTMORE SPRITES, CREATED BY FRANK LLOYD WRIGHT AND SCULPTOR ALFONSO IANELLI IN 1914, ARE SET ON THE HOTEL'S GROUNDS.

a conference center with a glorious stained glass ceiling was added, along with the Valley Wing, which holds another 120 rooms. Three years later, the Terrace Court was completed, bringing the total number of guest rooms at the Biltmore to more than 500. All of the hotel's major renovations were supervised by Taliesin Associated Architects of the Frank Lloyd Wright Foundation to ensure that they would complement the original structures on which Wright had worked.

The Biltmore, of course, offers more than just the genius of Frank Lloyd Wright. Seventeen tennis courts, three heated pools, two championship golf courses, a state-of-the-art exercise room and spa, and many fine shops and boutiques make the Arizona Biltmore a

▲ IN THE 1940S, MOVIE STAR CLARK GABLE *(SECOND FROM RIGHT)* AND HIS PARTY POSED FOR THE CAMERAMAN DURING A ROUND OF GOLF AT THE ARIZONA BILTMORE.

► MANY OF THE HOTEL'S FURNISHINGS, LIKE THE ONES IN THIS SUITE, WERE DESIGNED BY FRANK LLOYD WRIGHT.

resort hotel of the finest order.

The Biltmore also features four restaurants. The Gold Room, with its royal gold leaf ceiling, has been the hotel's main dining room since the resort opened. Patrons can also enjoy gourmet cuisine in the award-winning Orangerie, with its handsome chandeliers and a bank of greenhouse windows. The Café Sonora features an informal atmosphere and serves Southwestern specialties. And the poolside Cabana Club offers thirst-quenching concoctions, salads, and sandwiches. In addition, the Biltmore has two lounges for guests who wish to enjoy a cocktail after a day in the Arizona sun—the Orangerie Lounge and the Loggia, the lobby bar.

The Arizona Biltmore is owned by Equitable Life Assurance Society and is managed by Westin Hotels and Resorts. Affectionately called the "Jewel of the Desert," this splendid Arizona oasis facing Camelback Mountain offers sunbelt vacationers and business travelers a comfortable place in the sun as well as an introduction to an American architectural genius.

THE CATALINA POOL, PICTURED HERE,
IS ONE OF THE BILTMORE'S THREE
HEATED SWIMMING POOLS.

Caesars Palace
Las Vegas, Nevada

IF PITTSBURGH IS "THE STEEL CITY" and New Orleans is "the jazz city," then Las Vegas could rightly be called "the hotel city." This desert town set in Nevada's southeast corner is an oasis of neon lights and glitter created mainly to satisfy Americans' need for games of chance. Its main features are grand, action-packed gambling casinos and the hotels built to lodge those who need an occasional break from the gaming tables. The most famous hostelry in this city of hotels is Caesars Palace, a palazzo of pleasure and luxury set on the Las Vegas Strip, the string of glimmering hotels and casinos at the heart of town.

Caesars Palace— the apostrophe is omitted with apologies to grammarians—is a relative newcomer to Las Vegas. The city grew up just after World War II, when Benjamin "Bugsy" Siegel came to town and built the Flamingo, a neon-lighted hotel-casino that featured round-the-clock gambling, glitzy lounges and eateries, and scantily clad showgirls. Caesars, which opened on August 5, 1966, was founded by Jay Sarno, a hotelier who owned the famous Cabana Hotel in

▲ As THIS CORRIDOR SUGGESTS, DECOR AND ARTWORK IN THE MANNER OF ANCIENT ROME ARE FEATURED THROUGHOUT THE HOTEL COMPLEX.

◀ THE SWIMMING POOL AND SPA COMPLEX FEATURES AN OLYMPIC-SIZE SWIMMING POOL AND THE SHALLOWER TANNING POOL PICTURED HERE.

Palo Alto, California, and designed by Melvin Grossman, a Miami architect. The new hotel comprised 680 guest rooms; the large Colosseum Convention Complex; two restaurants; a swimming pool with spa; the Roman Forum Casino; and the 980-seat Circus Maximus Showroom, a nightclub that promised to attract the best talent in show business.

At its opening, Caesars Palace was impressive, even by Las Vegas' standards, but additions over the ensuing 25 years have made the hotel the centerpiece of the Las Vegas Strip.

During the 1970s, three high-rise towers were added, giving Caesars more than 1,500 guest rooms and suites. Two more casinos, the Olympic and the Palace Court, were eventually built, and the dome-shaped and dome-screened Omnimax Theater opened late in 1979. In 1983, the hotel added the Villa Suites, a group of 14 luxury chambers named after ancient Roman noblemen, furnished with crushed velvet sofas and circular beds, and equipped with private saunas and Jacuzzis. Today Caesars

houses nine restaurants catering to a wide variety of tastes, from the elegant Palace Court, with its crystal-and-bronze round elevator and bronze-balustraded spiral staircase, to the informal Café Roma, which serves both light snacks and complete meals. The Spanish Steps Steak and Seafood House, the AhSo, La Piazza Food Court and Lounge, and the Primavera offer Caesars diners an array of international delights.

Caesars Palace is designed to resemble a luxurious Roman palace. The hotel-casino complex is fronted by a series of brightly lit fountains, flanked by magnificent Roman archways. Within the palace walls is the Garden of the Gods. On the first level is an Olympic-size swimming pool and deck, inlaid with imported marble and surrounded by marble columns topped with etched-glass lighting panels. The second level features a smaller and shallower tanning pool and a circular spa with a waterfall whose contents cascade into the marble pool below. A carefully

landscaped courtyard flanks the complex, calling to mind the elegant gardens of ancient Rome. Roman statuary is also abundant throughout the hotel. Among the most impressive pieces is the Quadriga, a gold-leaf chariot, complete with horses and charioteer, which guards the arches fronting the Olympic Casino.

ONE OF THE HOTEL'S MAIN ATTRACTIONS is the World of Caesar, a rotunda-shaped structure set in a lush Roman garden and guarded by a marble statue of Apollo, the Greek and Roman god of music, poetry, and prophesy. A costumed centurion stationed at the attraction's ornate brass doors greets visitors and

THE CLEOPATRA SUITE, PICTURED HERE, IS ONE OF CAESARS' MANY LUXURY SUITES, OFFERING SOME OF THE MOST ELEGANT ACCOMMODATIONS IN LAS VEGAS.

◄ MOST PEOPLE COME TO THE LAS VEGAS STRIP FOR ITS GAMBLING CASINOS, LIKE THE ONE PICTURED HERE IN CAESARS.

► LUCILLE BALL *(SECOND FROM RIGHT)* AND FAMILY DINE AT CAESARS' BACCHANAL RESTAURANT.

FOUNTAINS AND STATUARY MODELED AFTER ANCIENT GREEK AND ROMAN SCULPTURES ARE LOCATED THROUGHOUT THE HOTEL.

directs them to the magical world inside—a miniature city of Rome as it probably looked during the time of Augustus Caesar. Carefully crafted model buildings are set in an authentic-looking landscape. A moving walkway takes the visitors on a tour of "the Eternal City." Landmarks like the Colosseum and the Forum are highlighted, and a miniature Caesar and Cleopatra speak and move about in their royal palace. A laser sound system and other special effects give guests the impression that they have have just stepped back in time 2,000 years.

Another Caesars attraction, one that appeals to guests with a taste for more than ancient history, is Cleopatra's Barge, a floating cocktail lounge designed to resemble an ancient Egyptian pleasure boat. Inside, a large dance floor and contemporary music invite guests to kick up their heels. The ship's deck actually rocks gently when the dancers get moving.

Despite its ancient Roman decor, Caesars Palace is a state-of-the-art hotel and casino offering patrons all the comforts and conveniences of the late 20th century. Many of the guest rooms include whirlpool baths, remote-control televisions, and other amenities. The hotel offers parking for more than 1,500 vehicles. People Movers transport patrons into the complex, which also features tennis courts, a beauty salon, and elegant shops. The Olympiad Race and Sports Book presents computerized wagering information on sports events throughout the country.

THESE GLITTERING FACILITIES, however, are not Caesars' only attraction. Many guests visit the hotel to see some of the world's best performers play the Circus Maximus Showroom. Andy Williams, Diana Ross, Joan Rivers, and Willie Nelson are just a few of those who have headlined at Caesars over the years, and athletes such as Muhammad Ali, Jimmy Connors, Mary Lou Retton, and Katarina Witt have also demonstrated their skills. On New Year's Eve in 1967, Evel Knievel tried to jump his motorcycle across Caesars' fountains. He was unsuccessful, but more than 21 years later, his son Robbie performed the feat.

Many sports fans also know Caesars Palace as the site of many of the best boxing matches of the past 25 years. Since he won the welterweight title at the hotel on November 30, 1979, "Sugar Ray" Leonard has fought some of his greatest bouts here. On September 16, 1981, for example, he bested Thomas "Hit Man" Hearns with a stunning 14th-round knockout; and on April 6, 1987, he upset "Marvelous Marvin" Hagler before a Caesars audience in the fight with the largest purse in boxing history.

After a quarter century of operation, Caesars Palace, owned by Caesars World Inc., has become a Las Vegas landmark. In a city known for its bright lights and glimmering night spots, none shines more vibrantly than this Roman palazzo.

CAESARS PALACE IS FRONTED BY BRIGHTLY LIT FOUNTAINS. IN THE FOREGROUND OF THIS PICTURE IS A COPY OF *VICTORY OF THE SAMOTHRACE.* THE ORIGINAL IS IN THE LOUVRE IN PARIS.

The Mark Hopkins Inter-Continental Hotel
San Francisco, California

• • •

SAN FRANCISCO, founded in the 1770s by Mexican explorers, grew up in the 1850s, when California gold rushers built shacks at the base of Nob Hill and merchants set up shops to serve the miners and their families. After the Civil War, when railroads connected California with the rest of America, San Francisco became an important west coast commercial and shipping center. In 1906, the city was nearly destroyed by one of the most severe earthquakes on record, but San Francisco's civic and business leaders vowed to clear the rubble and rebuild their town in short order. The reconstruction effort turned San Francisco into one of the world's great cities.

The portion of Nob Hill occupied by the Mark Hopkins Inter-Continental Hotel embraces the entire history of San Francisco. The hotel is named after a merchant who arrived in the wake of the great Gold Rush and became a successful shopkeeper, earning enough to get started in the lucrative railroad business. With three partners, Hopkins formed the Central Pacific Railroad, which, together

▲ THE MARK HOPKINS' LOBBY IS APPOINTED WITH RICH PATTERNED CARPETING, CRYSTAL CHANDELIERS, AND HANDSOME EASY CHAIRS.

◄ THE 19-STORY MARK HOPKINS HOTEL, LOCATED ON SAN FRANCISCO'S NOB HILL, OPENED IN 1926.

with the Union Pacific Railroad, forged the first transcontinental railway line in 1869. By the 1870s, Hopkins was a very wealthy man.

In around 1875, Hopkins purchased property on Nob Hill and commissioned the architectural firm of Wright and Saunders to build a mansion suitable for a successful businessman and his wife. The design was left to Mrs. Hopkins, and she and the architects created a grand 40-room castle in the Gothic style, with many turrets and gingerbread trim. But Hopkins died just before the home was completed. His widow moved in in 1878, but she remarried and moved east several years later. After she died in 1891, her second husband, Edward Searles, gave the Nob Hill mansion to the San Francisco Art Association, which converted it into a gallery and studios.

The fires that followed the 1906 earthquake—and destroyed nearly 500 blocks of San Francisco—consumed the Hopkins mansion, which was made of handsome but flammable California redwood. Thereafter, the Art Association erected an

THE LOWER BAR, WITH ITS ECHOES OF THE SEA IN AN ART DECO STYLE, SERVES COCKTAILS, SNACKS, AND AFTERNOON TEA.

undistinguished wooden building where Hopkins' magnificent home had stood. But according to legend, one evening in 1910, a Berkeley mining engineer named George D. Smith walked by the new art building and told a friend, "Someday, I'm going to build a hotel there."

Within ten years, Smith had become chairman of the State Industrial Commission and had made a start in the hotel business. He bought, refurbished, and sold the old Biltmore Hotel in San Francisco and built and managed the Hotel Canterbury. In 1925, he purchased the art building that he had strolled by 15 years earlier and began planning a large luxury hotel. Two San Francisco architects, Peter Weeks and William P. Day, were enlisted to design the hostelry, and the result—the Mark Hopkins Hotel—opened on December 4, 1926.

WEEKS AND DAY'S creation in no way resembled the Gothic mansion that had once stood in its place. The new hotel on Nob Hill was a sleek, modern structure that combined the style of the Spanish Renaissance with that of a French château. The 19-story central tower sat catty-corner to the intersection of California and Mason Streets, and two large wings angled away from the entranceway—a design that afforded each guest room a spectacular view of San Francisco Bay and the surrounding area. The hotel's facade was embellished with terra-cotta ornamentation, and a splendid arched entranceway fronted the building, leading patrons to

THE TOP OF THE MARK RESTAURANT, ON THE HOTEL'S TOP FLOOR, OFFERS DINERS A PANORAMIC VIEW OF SAN FRANCISCO. THE FAMED TRANSAMERICA BUILDING CAN BE SEEN ON THE LEFT IN THIS PICTURE.

The Beverly Hills Hotel
Los Angeles, California

IN 1906, when Burton Green, president of the Rodeo Land and Water Company, purchased 12 acres of land in Rancho de Las Aguas, California, he hoped that oil lay just beneath its surface. When extensive drilling proved him wrong, however, Green changed plans. He renamed his acreage "Beverly Hills," after his home in Beverly Farms, Massachusetts, and decided to build a luxury hotel on the site.

It was a bold move, for at the turn of the century Green's property was literally in the middle of nowhere; it was located near a hamlet of 500 residents, 10 miles west of downtown Los Angeles and 7 miles from the ocean. Green believed, however, that the lima bean fields surrounding his acreage could eventually be turned into high-priced real estate. Of course, Green guessed correctly. Despite the lack of oil, Beverly Hills

turned into one of America's wealthiest suburbs, and Green's creation, the Beverly Hills Hotel, became one of the country's most extravagant hostelries.

▲ PHOTOS OF HOLLYWOOD STARS ADORN THE WALLS OF THE MAIN DINING ROOM. MENU OFFERINGS INCLUDE JOHNNY CARSON'S WHITEFISH, ELIZABETH TAYLOR'S CHILI, AND FRANK SINATRA'S FAVORITE CHEESECAKE.

◀ THE BEVERLY HILLS HOTEL, LOCATED ON SUNSET BOULEVARD, IS AMONG THE TOWN'S MOST FAMOUS LANDMARKS. THE HOTEL OPENED IN 1912.

Green's hotel, which opened in 1912, was a grand stucco edifice, in the style of a southern California mission, with a score of adjoining bungalows.

Pink in color with tile roofs, the new hotel probably at first appeared too flashy for the surrounding area, but Green's development company financed gracefully curved streets and laid out estate-size lots to attract California's rich and famous to his neighborhood.

In 1920, Green sold his hotel to Margaret Anderson, his manager. Soon afterward, nearby Hollywood began to develop into the American motion picture capital, and its new celebrities—Charles Chaplin, Douglas Fairbanks, Buster Keaton, Rudolph Valentino—began acquiring Beverly Hills real estate and erecting large luxury homes. When the stars flocked to Beverly Hills, they stayed at Mrs. Anderson's hotel, which was strategically located at the intersection of Sunset Boulevard and Rodeo Drive.

In 1923, Will Rogers, the Oklahoma

cowboy-humorist, became honorary mayor of Beverly Hills, and he insisted that the inauguration take place on the grounds of the Beverly Hills Hotel. Charles Lindbergh, Orson Welles, Errol Flynn, W. C. Fields, John Barrymore—they all slept at the pink stucco lodge on Sunset Boulevard when they came to town. Clark Gable and Carole Lombard supposedly began their romance in one of the hotel's bungalows. Then the Depression hit and the hotel closed for two years, but it reopened in 1932, and as Hollywood enjoyed one of its most profitable decades, the Beverly Hills Hotel again became the place where the stars congregated.

One of the hotel's most famous—and least visible—guests was Howard Hughes. In 1942, the reclusive billionaire rented four of the hotel's bungalows—one for himself, one for his wife, actress Jean Peters, and two as decoys—and stayed, on and off, for the next 30 years. His quirky personality has spawned some of the hotel's classic stories. Not only did he routinely order meals at odd hours of the night, he once demanded that a roast beef sandwich be hidden in a palm tree near his bungalow so that he could obtain it undetected. He also handsomely paid orchestras to perform in the ballroom at four o'clock in the morning so that he could enjoy a private dance with a young Hollywood starlet.

In more recent years, the Beverly Hills has played host to Marilyn Monroe, Elizabeth Taylor and her several husbands, Warren Beatty, and Faye Dunaway. Dean Martin and Frank Sinatra reportedly used the hotel's Polo Lounge to cap off their raucous nights on the town. The hotel's guest register could probably be published as a "Who's Who in Hollywood."

BUT THE BEVERLY HILLS HOTEL offers more than a register filled with famous names. It has become a resplendent California oasis, a Spanish mission offering its guests sanctuary from the congested Los Angeles freeways. Everywhere on the hotel grounds are colorful gardens and flowering shrubs. A graceful arched promenade flanked by tall palm trees and neatly trimmed hedges leads to the hotel's main entryway. The airy lobby is informal yet tasteful, presenting the casual atmosphere and decor that Californians desire. Throughout the lobby and public rooms lush plants and striking floral arrangements bring the flavor of the outdoors indoors.

◄ THE HOTEL'S MOST POPULAR GUEST QUARTERS ARE THE 21 BUNGALOWS, SET APART FROM THE MAIN BUILDINGS TO ENSURE MUCH-COVETED PRIVACY. THIS IS BUNGALOW 5, NAMED FOR ELIZABETH TAYLOR.

THE ELITE OF BEVERLY HILLS TURNED OUT IN FORMAL ATTIRE FOR A FESTIVE AFFAIR AT THE BEVERLY HILLS SHORTLY AFTER THE HOTEL'S OPENING.

The 268 guest rooms and suites are elegantly appointed. Many have fireplaces, private patios, and terraces. All are equipped with color televisions and VCRs. The hotel complex also includes 21 bungalows. These cozy cottages, ranging in size from one to four bedrooms, are snugly nestled away among palm groves and colorful flower gardens, offering patrons luxury accommodations and highly coveted privacy.

The hotel's most popular outdoor area is undoubtedly the swimming pool and cabana complex. A patio of pink and beige Mexican *adoquin* stone surrounds the pool, and a Spanish fountain pours forth a cascade of fresh water. A heated whirlpool is nearby, and the Cabana Club Café serves poolside lunches and beverages.

THE BEVERLY HILLS HOTEL is also known for its fine restaurants. The main dining room offers California and French gourmet cuisine, including Johnny Carson's Whitefish, Elizabeth Taylor's Chili, Liza Minnelli's Salade de Provence, and Frank Sinatra's Favorite Cheesecake. The Polo Lounge, a favorite among celebrities, offers breakfast, lunch, afternoon tea, and dinner with musical accompaniment in an airy California setting, with private booths that overlook a garden patio. And the Fountain Coffee Shop, tucked away under the

A TABLE ON THE POLO LOUNGE PATIO IS ONE OF THE MOST COVETED LUNCH RESERVATIONS IN ALL OF BEVERLY HILLS.

THE HOTEL'S LOBBY IS SIMPLY FURNISHED AND DECORATED WITH LUSH PLANTS AND FLORAL ARRANGEMENTS. THE HOTEL'S OFFICIAL COLORS, PINK AND GREEN, CAN BE FOUND ON THE WALLS, CARPETS, FURNISHINGS, AND ART WORK.

Polo Lounge stairway, provides an informal atmosphere for hungry patrons. Meals are also served in the hotel's meeting rooms, which are often the setting for weddings, conferences, and benefits.

After more than 75 years of service, the Beverly Hills Hotel, now owned by Sajahtera, Incorporated, a subsidiary of the Brunei Investment Agency, has become the most recognizable landmark in one of America's most famous suburbs. Hollywood celebrities who own majestic mansions on Rodeo Drive may be seen driving on the streets of Beverly Hills in their Ferraris and Rolls-Royces, but perhaps the town's greatest star is a pink and green hotel on Sunset Boulevard.

THE BEVERLY HILLS HOTEL, BUILT IN THE STYLE OF A SOUTHERN CALIFORNIA MISSION, HAS WALLS MADE OF PINK STUCCO.

Hotel del Coronado
Coronado, California

◆ ◆ ◆

WHEN TOURISTS LODGED at the Hotel del Coronado during the 1890s, they viewed the inn as a cultural oasis, a splash of civilization in the untamed American West. The southern coast of California was still rugged and virtually uncharted then, and the Coronado's visitors were thankful for a respite from a dusty wagon ride or a cramped railroad car.

"The Del," as the Hotel del Coronado has come to be known, was conceived by Elisha Babcock, Jr., a railroad magnate, and his close friend, H. L. Story, the chief executive of the Story and Clark Piano Company of Chicago. During the early 1880s, the two Midwestern business tycoons had been spending their vacations hunting the wild Coronado Peninsula on San Diego Bay. While enjoying the splendid view and the gentle Mediterranean climate of southern

California, Babcock and Story began to consider the rich possibilities for development offered by such a marvelous slice of real estate. The weather

▲ THE HOTEL'S STAFF, WHICH INCLUDES UPHOLSTERERS AND WOODWORKERS, INSURE THE MAINTENANCE AND PRESERVATION OF THE DEL'S MANY ANTIQUE FURNISHINGS.

◀ THE HOTEL DEL CORONADO, A SPLENDID EXAMPLE OF VICTORIAN SEASIDE ARCHITECTURE, OPENED IN 1888.

was splendid year round, the hunting and fishing were extraordinary, and the ocean views were magnificent. Moreover, the two savvy businessmen surmised that the San Diego region,

still remote and unsettled, would eventually become a center for tourism and commerce.

In 1885, when the transcontinental railroad arrived about 150 miles north of San Diego, Babcock and Story purchased 4,100 acres of land on the Coronado Peninsula and began making plans for a grand hotel and resort. They enlisted the Reid Brothers of Evansville, Indiana, Babcock's hometown, to design a place that would be the "talk of the Western World." Although the Reids had designed only railroad stations until that time, they conceived one of America's finest examples of the extravagant seaside hotel.

Construction began in March 1887. Masons, carpenters, plumbers, craftsmen, and hundreds of unskilled Chinese laborers were transported by boat from San Francisco and Oakland to work on Babcock and Story's dream. A

kiln was built for making bricks, and the San Diego Granite Company was charged with providing rock from nearby quarries. Quality china was shipped from France, glassware from Belgium, and furniture and carpeting from Massachusetts. The Hotel del Coronado held its formal opening on February 19, 1888, only 11 months after construction began.

T HE HOTEL DEL CORONADO'S first guests saw a rambling structure in the fashionable Queen Anne style of the day. An enormous rotunda slit with long, narrow windows flanked the hotel's formal entrance hall and housed an impressive grand ballroom. An eclectic collection of turrets, towers, and cupolas and a wide range of building materials—wood, shingle, glass, brick—suggested the spontaneity of the Victorian age. The building itself was constructed with wood, covered with immaculate white paint, and topped with a red shingle roof. The hotel surrounded a garden patio with lush tropical plants imported from around the world.

Inside, the main entranceway opened to the Grand Lobby, tastefully decorated with Victorian furniture and accents. Flanking the lobby were the Grand Ballroom and the Crown Room,

◀ THE LOBBY'S COMFORTABLE SOFAS AND EASY CHAIRS, PATTERNED CARPETS, ELEGANT CHANDELIERS, AND IMMACULATELY POLISHED WOODWORK RE-CREATE THE 1890S FOR CONTEMPORARY GUESTS.

THIS BATHROOM HAS BEEN RESTORED TO ITS ORIGINAL VICTORIAN STYLE.

the hotel's formal dining hall. Corridors and stairways led to 400 rooms, many of which offered spectacular views of San Diego Bay and the sandy beach along its shores. Rooms could be rented for the outrageous rate of $2.00 per night!

A CENTURY HAS PASSED since the Hotel del Coronado's formal opening, and the facilities have been greatly expanded and carefully restored. Additions now house another 300 rooms, giving the Del a total of nearly 700. Preservation experts and skilled craftsmen are retained to ensure that the continual job of modernization does not compromise the hotel's original splendor.

The contemporary guests who stay at the Del still see it in much the same way as the lodgers did a century ago. But today the hotel offers travelers an escape from the hectic world of highways and workplace. Guests can experience the opulence of the Victorian era while still enjoying the luxuries of the late 20th century—lighted tennis courts, spacious swimming pools, state-of-the-art spas and fitness centers, quality gifts shops, and fashionable salons.

Today's travelers who stop at the Del after a stressful day on the California freeways enter a magical kingdom by the sea, a grand castle flanked by a marina, golf course, and clean beaches. An attentive staff, specially trained to provide expert service, pampers the Del's patrons and keeps its facilities in superb condition. Its eateries—the lavish Crown Room and the Prince of Wales Restaurant—offer gourmet fare

◀ THE CROWN ROOM, PICTURED HERE, HAS SERVED AS THE HOTEL'S FORMAL DINING ROOM FOR MORE THAN A CENTURY.

▶ APPROPRIATELY THE CAMERAMAN CAUGHT UP WITH AQUATIC MOVIE STAR ESTHER WILLIAMS AND HER TWO SONS ON THE BEACH AT THE CORONADO DEL MAR. THE PHOTO WAS TAKEN DURING THE 1950S.

and extensive wine lists. Its comfortable lounges—the Lobby Bar and the Ocean Terrace—provide the visitor with the perfect setting for socializing and sipping cocktails. After a three-day respite at the Hotel del Coronado, few guests are anxious to return to the office.

Perhaps contemporary travelers are drawn to the Del, in part, by the chance to catch a glimpse of the hotel's many celebrity guests. Twelve United

States presidents have stayed there; the first was Benjamin Harrison in 1891, the most recent, George Bush. Perhaps the most famous European notable to visit the Del was the Prince of Wales— later King Edward VIII—who, 16 years after his 1920 visit, abdicated his throne to marry American socialite Wallis Simpson. Other visitors have included Hollywood stars like Greta Garbo, Mae West, Van Johnson, and Jerry Lewis;

athletes like Jack Dempsey, Babe Ruth, and Chris Evert; and national heroes like Charles Lindbergh and Scott Carpenter. *Some Like It Hot*, the Billy Wilder film starring Marilyn Monroe, Jack Lemmon, and Tony Curtis, was filmed in part at the Coronado, as was *The Stunt Man*, the 1979 movie featuring Peter O'Toole.

The Hotel del Coronado, designated a National Historic Landmark in 1977, is presently owned by the Hotel del Coronado Corporation, chaired by M. Larry Lawrence. Besides serving as a luxury vacation spot for California travelers, the Del offers facilities for large conventions and hosts a variety of charitable events. The Coronado Peninsula has been tamed and settled, but its grand hotel still offers guests the splendid setting and service coveted by California travelers more than a century ago.

THE PALM COURT PROVIDES PATRONS WITH A GRAND VIEW OF THE COLORFUL GARDEN PATIO.

(*PHOTO ON PAGE 128*) A SITTING ROOM IN THE GREENBRIER, WHITE SULPHUR SPRINGS, WEST VIRGINIA.

The producers of this book gratefully acknowledge the assistance of the following individuals: Sarah Suggs, Barbara Worth of the Arizona Biltmore; Sheila O'Brien of the Beverly Hills Hotel; Gretchen DeWeese of the Breakers; Jane Andrade of the Brown Palace Hotel; Deborah Munch, Richard Gubbe, Margaret Kurtz of Caesars Palace; Joann Bongiorno of the Drake Hotel; Paul Brown of the Grand Hotel; Sharon Rowe of the Greenbrier; Nancy Weisinger, Judith Bond of the Hotel del Coronado; Gabriela Knubis of Knubis Advertising, Public Relations; Debbie Icard of the Mark Hopkins Inter-Continental Hotel; Faire Hart of the Mohonk Mountain House; John Olsen, Brad Harbach, Jean Donaldson of the Old Faithful Inn; Elizabeth Maguire of the Plaza; Brad Conner of the Seelbach Hotel; and Ann McCracken of the Willard Inter-Continental Hotel.